KU KLUX KLAN

A Da Capo Press Reprint Series

CIVIL LIBERTIES IN AMERICAN HISTORY

GENERAL EDITOR: LEONARD W. LEVY
Claremont Graduate School

KU KLUX KLAN

Its Origin,
Growth, and Disbandment

By J. C. Lester and D. L. Wilson

Introduction and Notes by
Walter L. Fleming

DA CAPO PRESS • NEW YORK • 1973

Library of Congress Cataloging in Publication Data

Lester, John C.
    Ku Klux Klan; its origin, growth, and disbandment.

    (Civil liberties in American history)
    Reprint of the 1905 ed.
    1. Ku Klux Klan. I. Wilson, Daniel Love,
1849-1902, joint author. II. Title. III. Series.
E668.L64   1973   322.4'2'0973   71-114758
ISBN 0-306-71927-4

This Da Capo Press edition of *Ku Klux Klan* is an
unabridged republication of the second edition, enlarged,
published in New York and Washington, D.C., in 1905.

Da Capo Press, Inc.
A Subsidiary of Plenum Publishing Corporation
227 West 17th Street, New York, New York 10011

Manufactured in the United States of America

KU KLUX KLAN

Ku Klux Klan

ITS ORIGIN, GROWTH AND DISBANDMENT

BY

J. C. LESTER AND D. L. WILSON

WITH

APPENDICES CONTAINING THE PRESCRIPTS
OF THE KU KLUX KLAN, SPECIMEN
ORDERS AND WARNINGS

WITH

INTRODUCTION AND NOTES

BY

WALTER L. FLEMING, PH. D.

*Professor of History in West Virginia University; Author
of "Civil War and Reconstruction in Alabama."*

———

NEW YORK AND WASHINGTON
THE NEALE PUBLISHING COMPANY
1905

NOTE OF ACKNOWLEDGMENT.

Assistance was given to me while searching for information in regard to Ku Klux Klan, by many former members of the order, and by their friends and relatives. Of especial value were the details given to me by Major James R. Crowe, of Sheffield, Alabama; the late Ryland Randolph, Esq., and his son, Ryland Randolph, Jr., of Birmingham, Alabama; Judge Z. T. Ewing, of Pulaski, Tennessee; Miss Cora R. Jones, of Birmingham, Alabama, niece of one of the founders of the Klan; Mr. Lacy H. Wilson, of Bristol, Tennessee, the son of one of the authors of the History printed within, Major S. A. Cunningham and Mr. A. V. Goodpasture, of Nashville, and Dr. John A. Wyeth, of New York City.

There is still much that is obscure about Ku Klux Klan and I shall be glad to obtain additional information in regard to the order, and also to receive notice of mistakes and errors in this account.

W. L. F.

CONTENTS

INTRODUCTION.

BY WALTER L. FLEMING.

PAGE

KU KLUX KLAN.

BY J. C. LESTER AND D. L. WILSON.

PAGE

APPENDICES.

PAGE

ILLUSTRATIONS

"When laws become lawless contrivances to defeat the ends of justice, it is not surprising that the people resort to lawless expedients for securing their rights."
—*S. S. Cox, in "Three Decades," p. 558.*

INTRODUCTION
BY
WALTER L. FLEMING

INTRODUCTION.

By Walter L. Fleming, Ph. D.,

Professor of History in West Virginia University.

Twenty-one years ago there was privately printed in Nashville, Tennessee, a little book by J. C. Lester and D. L. Wilson, that purported to be an account, from inside information, of the great secret order of Reconstruction days, known to the public as Ku Klux Klan. It attracted little notice then; and since that time it has not been given the attention it deserved as a historical document.[1] At the time of writing, sectional feeling was still inflamed; the Northern people were not ready to hear anything favorable about the Ku Klux Klan, which they considered a band of outlaws and murderers; and the Southern people were not desirous of being reminded of the dreadful Reconstruction period. Many of the members of the Klan who had been hunted for their

---

[1] Cutler, in his "Lynch Law," p. 139, is the first writer outside of the South who has paid serious attention to this history of Ku Klux Klan.

lives, and who were still technically outlawed, were unwilling to make known
their connection with the order and some
even considered their oaths still binding.
But since the book was printed, the
Prescripts or Constitutions of the order
have come to light, and the ex-members
are now generally willing to tell all they
know about the organization. As yet, no
other member has written an account of
the Klan, though several have been projected, and Lester and Wilson's History
seems likely to remain the only one written
altogether from inside sources.

The authors, Capt. John C. Lester and
Rev. D. L. Wilson, were in 1884, when the
booklet was written, residents in Pulaski,
Tennessee, where the first Den of the Klan
was founded. Major Lester was one of
the six original members of the Pulaski
Den or Circle. He made a fine record as
a soldier in the Civil War in the Third
Tennessee (Confederate) Infantry, and
afterwards became a lawyer and an official
in the Methodist Church, and was a member of the Tennessee legislature at the
time of writing the book. Rev. D. L.
Wilson, who put the account into its present form, was born in 1849, in Augusta

County, Virginia. He went to school to
Jed Hotchkiss and was graduated as val-
edictorian of his class from Washington
and Lee University, in 1873, and a year
later from the Union Theological Seminary, near Hampden-Sidney, Virginia.
From 1874 to 1880 he was pastor of a
Presbyterian church at Broadway, Virginia, and from 1880 to 1902 he served
a church in Pulaski, Tennessee. He died
in 1902 after a six months' residence in
Bristol, Tennessee, as pastor of the First
Presbyterian Church. He was not a
member of the Klan, but was acquainted
with the founders and with many other
former members, and had access to all the
records of the order that had not been
destroyed. In addition to information
received from other members, Wilson
was assisted by Captain Lester, who furnished most of the facts used, revised the
manuscript and the book was printed with
both names on the title page.

As a general account of the Ku Klux
movement Lester and Wilson's History
leaves something to be desired. It is
colored too much by conditions in Tennessee. No knowledge is shown of other
organizations similar to Ku Klux Klan,

when in fact there were several other very important ones, such as the White Brotherhood, the White League, the Pale Faces, the Constitutional Union Guards, and one, the Knights of the White Camelia,[1] that was larger than the Klan and covered a wider territory. Then, too, in an attempt to make a moderate statement that would be generally accepted, the authors failed to portray clearly the chaotic social, economic and political conditions that caused the rise of such orders, and in endeavoring to condemn the acts of violence committed under cloak of the order they went too far in the direction of apologetic explanation. Consequently, the causes seem somewhat trivial and the results not very important.[2] It would seem from their account that after a partial success, the movement failed in

[1] The Constitution and Ritual of the Knights of the White Camelia have been printed in West Virginia University Documents relating to Reconstruction, No. 1.

[2] Tourgee's "Invisible Empire" gives the carpetbagger's view of the Ku Klux movement, and, though filled with worthless testimony from the Ku Klux Report, it shows a very clear conception of the real meaning of the movement and a correct appreciation of its results. The best later interpretation is that of Mr. William Garrott Brown in "The Lower South," Ch. 4.

Some Klansmen

1. D. L. Wilson, one of the authors of "Ku Klux Klan." 2. Major J. R. Crowe, one of the founders. 3. Captain John C. Lester, one of the founders. 4. General Albert Pike, chief judicial officer. 5. General W. J. Hardee 6. Calvin Jones, one of the founders. 7. Ryland Randolph.

its attempt to regulate society, and degenerated into general disorder. This is a superficial conclusion and is not concurred in by the survivors of the period and those who understand the conditions of that time. The remnants of such a secret, illegal order were certain to degenerate finally into violence, but before it reached this stage it had accomplished much good in reducing to order the social chaos.[1]

In view of the fact that the Lester and Wilson account does not mention names it will be of interest to examine the *personnel* of the original Pulaski Circle, out of which the Klan developed. (See p. 52). (There were six young men in the party that first began to meet in the fall and winter of 1865: (1) Captain John C. Lester, of whom something has been said. (2) Major James Richard Crowe, now of Sheffield, Alabama, who was a native of Pulaski and was educated at Waterbury Academy and Giles College. When the Civil War began he was studying law in Marion, Alabama, and enlisted at once in the Marion Rifles, Com-

---

[1] For a full account of its work in Alabama see Fleming's "Civil War and Reconstruction in Alabama," Ch. 21.

pany "G," Fourth Alabama Infantry. Later
he was transferred to the 35th Tennessee
Infantry.   He was in the battles of Man-
assas, Fort Donelson, Shiloh, Shelton's
Hill, White Farm, Richmond, Perrysville,
and others of less importance. Three
times he was severely wounded and twice
discharged for disability. He was captured
with Sam Davis and both were tried as
spies; Crowe was acquitted and Davis was
hanged.   He has held high rank in the
Masonic order and has been an official
in the Cumberland Presbyterian Church.
(3) John Kennedy, the only survivor of
the original six except Major Crowe.
He was a soldier in the 3rd Tennessee
Infantry during the Civil War, is a
Presbyterian, and an honored citizen of
Lawrenceburg, Tennessee. (4) Calvin
Jones, son of Judge Thomas M. Jones,
was a lawyer, and a member of the Epis-
copal Church.   He was Adjutant of the
32nd Tennessee Infantry during the Civil
War.   (5) Richard R. Reed was a lawyer, a Presbyterian, and during the war
had served in the 3rd Tennessee Infantry.
(6) Frank O. McCord was editor of
the *Pulaski Citizen,* a Methodist, and had
been a private soldier in the Confederate

service. Two others came in at the second or third meeting—Capt. J. L. Pearcy, later of Nashville, now of Washington, D. C., and James McCallum.[1] The founders were all of Scotch-Irish descent and most of them were Presbyterians.

In regard to the founding of the Pulaski Circle, Major J. R. Crowe says: "Frank O. McCord was elected Grand Cyclops, and James R. Crowe, Grand Turk. A committee composed of Richard R. Reed and Calvin Jones[2] was appointed to select a name for the organization. The Greek for *circle* was chosen. We called it Kuklos(Κυκλοσ), which was changed to Ku Klux afterward when the name was proposed to the Circle. John Kennedy suggested that we add another *K*, and the order was then called Ku Klux Klan. . . .

---

[1] Other well-known members of the Pulaski Den were: Captain Robert Mitchell, Captain Thomas McCoy, Dr. M. S. Waters, Dr. James Bowers, Milton Voorheis, C. P. Jones, Robert Martin, Dr. C. C. Abernathy, I. L. Shappard, Robert Shappard, J. L. Nelson, John Moore, F. M. Crawford, Alexander McKissick, W. H. Rose.

[2] Charles P. Jones, brother of Calvin Jones, joined later. He now lives in Birmingham, Alabama.

The mysterious lights seen floating about the ruins (See p. 61) presented a weird and uncanny appearance and filled the superstitious with dread of the place; so we were never disturbed, and it only required a quaint garb and a few mysterious sounds to convince the uninitiated that we were spirits from the other world. We were quick to catch on to this idea and we governed ourselves accordingly. . . . During our parades or appearances in public the darkies either hid out or remained close in their houses. . . . The origin of the order had no political significance. It was at first purely social and for our amusement. It proved a great blessing to the entire South and did what the State and Federal officials could not do—it brought order out of chaos and peace and happiness to our beloved South. . . . The order was careful in the admission of members and I have never known of a betrayal of the secrets of the order. I am proud to say that I never knew of one single act done by the genuine Ku Klux Klan that I am ashamed of or do not now endorse."

Major Crowe and other members repeatedly mention the fact that the membership of the Klan was largely of Scotch-Irish descent. This was bound to be the case since in the territory covered by the Klan proper the great majority of the Scotch-Irish of the South were settled. The Ku Klux Klan extended from Virginia to Mississippi through the white county section—the Piedmont and mountain region. It seldom extended into the Black Belt, though it was founded on its borders. There another similar order—the Knights of the White Camelia—held sway. In the Piedmont region before the spread of the Klan, there were numerous secret protective societies among the whites, and these were later absorbed into the Klan. The Klan led a more strenuous existence than the Black Belt orders. In most of its territory, social conditions were worse than in the black counties. It is a mistake to consider that in 1865-1870, the whites in the densest black districts were in the place of greatest danger. There the blacks were usually the best behaved; there the whites were never divided and never lost their grip on society; there the negro still respected the white people as

beings almost superhuman. But race
relations were worse in the white districts where there was a lower class of
whites, some of whom mistreated the
negro and others encouraged him to violence. Here the negro had never had the
great respect for *all* whites that the Black
Belt negro had, and here the whites were
somewhat divided among themselves.
During the war the "tories," so called, or
those who claimed to be Union sym-
pathizers and the Confederates, alter-
nately mistreated one another, and the
close of the war brought no peace to
such communities. To this region escaped the outlaws, deserters, etc., of both
armies during the war, and here the
wreckage of war was worst. Such was
the nature of the country where the Klan
flourished. It was a kind of ex-Confederate protest against the doings of the
"tories," Unionists and outlaws, and the
negroes banded in the Union League.
For several years neither the Federal
Government nor the State Government
gave protection to the ex-Confederates
of this region, and naturally secret asso-

ciations were formed for self-defense. This method of self-defense is as old as history.[1]

The members of Ku Klux Klan are nowadays inclined to consider that their order comprehended all that took shape in resistance to the Africanization of society and government during the Reconstruction period. As one ex-member said: "Nearly all prominent men—ex-Confederates—in all the Southern states were connected in some way with the Klan." This is true only indirectly. Nearly all white men, it may be said, took part in the movement now called the "Ku Klux Movement." But more of them belonged to other organizations than were members of the Klan. The Klan had the most striking name and it was later applied to the whole movement. The more prominent pol-

---

[1] Examples in European history are the Carbonari of Italy, the Tugenbund and the Vehmgericht of Germany, the Klephts of Greece, Young Italy, the Nihilists of Russia, the Masonic order in most Catholic countries during the first half of the Nineteenth Century, Beati Paoli of Sicily, the Illuminati, etc. The "Confréries" of Medieval France were similar illegal societies formed "pour défendre les innocentes et reprimer les violences iniques."—Lavisse et Rambaud, Histoire Generale, Vol. 2, p. 466.

iticians, it is said, had no direct connection with any such orders. Such connection would have embarrassed and hampered them in their work, but most of them were in full sympathy with the objects of the Ku Klux movement, and profited by its successes. Many of the genuine Unionists later joined in the movement, and there were some few negro members, I have been told. Some prominent men were honorary members, so to speak, of the order. They sympathized with its objects, and gave advice and encouragement, but were not initiated and did not take active part. General John B. Gordon, of Georgia, and General W. J. Hardee, of Alabama, were such members. The active members were, as a rule, young men. In this respect the Klan differed from the order of White Camelia, which discouraged the initiation of very young men.

Some well-known members of the Klan were General John C. Brown, of Pulaski, Tennessee; Captain John W. Morton, now Secretary of State of Tennessee; Ryland Randolph, of Tuscaloosa, Alabama, editor of the *Independent Monitor,* the official organ of the Klan in Alabama; General N. B. Forrest and General George

W. Gordon, of Memphis, Tennessee;
Generals John B. Gordon, A. H. Colquitt,
G. T. Anderson and A. R. Lawton, of
Georgia; General W. J. Hardee, of Alabama; Colonel Joseph Fussell, of Columbia, Tennessee. General Albert Pike,
who stood high in the Masonic order, was
the chief judicial officer of the Klan.

General Forrest heard of the order
after it began to spread, and after investigation consented to become its head as
Grand Wizard. He was initiated by
Captain John W. Morton, who had formerly been his chief of artillery. Under
him the order, which was becoming de-
moralized, was reorganized. As soon as
it had done its work he disbanded it. An
enterprising newspaper reporter inter-
viewed General Forrest, in 1868, on
the subject of Ku Klux Klan and ex-
tracted much information;[1] but when
before the Ku Klux Committee of Congress, in 1871, the General would make
only general statements and he evaded
some of the interrogatories. To the
committee he appeared to be wonderfully
familiar with the principles of the order,
but very ignorant as to details. The

---

[1] See Ku Klux Report, Vol. 13, p. 32.

average member of Congress, ignorant of Southern conditions, did not understand that the members of the order considered themselves bound by the supreme oath of the Klan and that other oaths, if in conflict with it, were not binding. That is, the ex-Confederates under the command of Forrest, Grand Wizard of the Invisible Empire, were obeying the first law of nature and were bound to reveal nothing to injure the cause, just as when Confederates under Forrest, Lieutenant-General of the Confederate Army, they were bound not to reveal military information to the hostile forces. The government, in their view, had not only failed to protect them, but was being used to oppress them. Consequently they were disregarding its claim to obedience.

Now that General Forrest's connection with the Klan is known it is amusing to read the testimony he gave before the Ku Klux Committee of Congress in 1871.[1] Though evading questions aimed to elicit definite information, yet he was willing to speak of the general conditions that caused the development of the organ-

---

[1] Ku Klux Report, Vol. 13, Florida and Miscellaneous, p. 3.

GENERAL N. B. FORREST

Grand Wizard of Ku Klux Klan

ization in Tennessee. He stated that it
was meant as a defensive organization
among the Southern whites to offset the
work of the Union League, which had
organized, armed and drilled the negroes,
and had committed numerous outrages
on the whites; to protect ex-Confederates from extermination by Brownlow's
"loyal" militia; to prevent the burning
by negroes of gins, mills, dwellings, and
villages, which was becoming common;
to protect white women from criminal
negro men; in short to make life and
property safe and keep the South from
becoming a second San Domingo. He
stated that about the time the order arose
he was getting as many as fifty letters a
day from his old soldiers who were
suffering under the disordered conditions
that followed the war, whose friends and
relatives were being murdered, whose
wives and daughters were being insulted,
etc. They wanted advice and assistance
from him. Not being able to write himself, on account of a wounded shoulder,
he kept a secretary busy answering such
letters. Most of the defensive bodies,
Forrest stated, had no names and had no
connection with one another. He admit-

ted that he had belonged to the Pale Faces, and that he fully approved of the objects of the Klan. A copy of the original Prescript was shown to him and he was able to say that he had never seen it before. In his day, the Revised and Amended Prescript was used, which was never discovered by any investigating committee. He maintained that the order was careful in admitting new members, only sober, mature, discreet gentlemen being allowed to join. At one time, Forrest estimated, so a newspaper reporter stated, that the Klan had 40,000 members in Tennessee and 550,000 in the entire South. This estimate was probably not exaggerated if the entire membership of all the orders similar to the Klan be counted in. Forrest refused to give the names of members. It is likely, from several bits of evidence, that he had much to do with consolidating the order, giving it a military organization, and making its work effective.

General John B. Gordon, the most prominent military man, next to Forrest, who was connected with the Klan, gave a clear account of the conditions in Georgia that led to the organization of the defensive societies of whites.[1] In Georgia the state of affairs where General Gordon lived was in some respects unlike conditions in Tennessee. In Tennessee the whites were somewhat divided among themselves and there were not so many blacks. In Georgia, according to Gordon, the principal danger was from blacks, incited to hostility and violence by alien whites of low character. The latter organized the negroes into armed Union Leagues, taught them that the whites were hostile to all their rights, and that the lands of the whites were to be, or ought to be, divided among the blacks. Under such influences the negroes who had not made trouble began to show signs of restlessness; some of them banded together to plunder the whites, and serious crimes became frequent, especially that of rape, and men were afraid to leave their families in order to attend to their business. The whites feared a general insurrection of the blacks, and as Gordon stated, "if the sort of teachings given [to the negroes] in Georgia had been carried out to its logical results the negroes would

---

[1] See Ku Klux Report, Georgia Testimony, p. 304.

have slaughtered whole neighborhoods."
That they did not do so, was, in his
opinion, due to the forbearance and self-
control of the whites, and to the natural
kindness and good disposition of the
negroes and their remembrance of former
pleasant relations with the whites. There
was no great danger, as one can see today,
of the negro uprisings, but the whites
thought then that there was. The relig-
ious frenzy of the blacks during the year
after the war also alarmed the whites.
The black troops stationed in Georgia
were frequently guilty of gross outrages
against white citizens and were a constant
incitement to violence on the part of their
fellow blacks. The carpetbag government pardoned and turned loose upon
society the worst criminals. There was
no law for several years. The whites
were subject to arbitrary arrest and trials
by drumhead courts-martial; military
prisoners were badly mistreated. In
general, society and government were in a
condition of anarchy; the white race was
disorganized, and the blacks organized,
but not for good purposes.

General Gordon spoke of another matter
often mentioned by the best class of

GENERAL JOHN B. GORDON

Head of Klan in Georgia

ex-Confederate soldiers: the Southern
soldier believed that the "Appomattox
Program" had not been carried out.
At Appomattox the magnanimity of General Grant and the victorious soldiers had
impressed very favorably the defeated
Confederates. The latter believed that if
Grant and the soldiers who had defeated
them had been allowed to settle matters,
there would have been no more trouble.
Instead, the politicians had taken charge
and had stirred up endless strife. No
effort at conciliation had been made; and
the magnanimity of Grant gave way to
the vindictive policies of politicians.[1]

---

[1] General Clanton, of Alabama, complained that
the Southern people had passed "out of the hands
of warriors into the hands of squaws." General
Edmund W. Pettus, now U. S. Senator from
Alabama, said that the entire Reconstruction was
in violation of the understanding made at the
surrender of the Confederate armies. The Confederate soldier surrendered with arms in hand
and in return a certain contract was made in his
parole according to which, as long as he was law-
abiding, he was not to be disturbed. This contract
had been violated. The government of the United
States had made a promise to men with arms in
their hands and had violated this promise by passing the Reconstruction measures, which amounted
to punishment of individuals for alleged crime
without trial by law. See Ku Klux Report,
Alabama Testimony, pp. 224, 377, 383.

The whites believed that the "understanding of Appomattox" had been violated and that they had been deliberately humiliated by the Washington government.

Such were some of the influences, in General Gordon's opinion, that caused the spread of the Klan in Georgia. He says that he heartily approved the objects of the order, that it was purely for self-protection, an organization for police purposes, a peace police, which kept the peace, prevented riots, and restrained the passionate whites as well as the violent blacks. Its membership was, he said, of the best citizens, mostly ex-Confederates, led by the instinct of self-preservation to band together. It was secret because the leaders were sure that the sympathy of the Federal Government would be against them and would consider a public organization a fresh rebellion. It took no part in politics and died out when the whites were able to obtain protection from the police and the courts.

These were the explanations of men who were high in the order but who never attended a meeting and were never in actual contact with its workings. Private

members—Ghouls they were called—could
have told more thrilling stories. But
deficient as the accounts of Gordon and
Forrest are in detail they supplement the
history of Lester and Wilson in explaining
the causes that lay at the bottom of the
secret revolution generally called the Ku
Klux Movement.

As to the success or failure of the movement, Lester and Wilson, condemning the
violence that naturally resulted from the
movement, cause the impression (Ch. 4)
that the main result was disorder. Such
was not the case, nor was it the intention
of the writers to create such an impression.
The important work of the Klan was
accomplished in regaining for the whites
control over the social order and in putting
them in a fair way to regain political control. In some States this occurred sooner
than in others. When the order accomplished its work it passed away. It was
formally disbanded before the evil results
of carpet bag governments could be seen.
When it went out of existence in 1869,
there had been few outrages, but its name
and prestige lived after it and served to
hide the evil deeds of all sorts and conditions of outlaws. But these could be

crushed by the government, State or Federal. In a wider and truer sense the phrase "Ku Klux Movement" means the attitude of Southern whites toward the various measures of Reconstruction lasting from 1865 until 1876, and, in some respects, almost to the present day.

Two elaborate Prescripts or Constitutions were adopted by the Ku Klux Klan —the original Prescript (See Appendix I) and the Revised and Amended Prescript (See Appendix II). The ritual and initiatory ceremonies and obligations were never printed. The by-laws and the ritual of the Pulaski Circle or Den were elaborate but were in manuscript only. They were quite absurd and were intended only to furnish amusement to the members at the expense of the candidates for initiation. No oaths were prescribed—only a pledge of secrecy. As the Klan spread among neighboring towns, the Pulaski by-laws and ritual were modified for the use of new Dens. After the Klan had changed character and become a body of regulators, and it was decided that the administration should be centralized, a convention of delegates from the Dens met in Nashville, in April, 1867, and adopted the original Prescript already referred to. Lester and Wilson are mistaken in saying (Ch. 3) that the Revised and Amended Prescript was adopted at this convention. Where and how this Prescript was printed no one now knows. A copy was sent, without notice or explanation, from Memphis to the Grand Cyclops of each Den. It must have been printed in a small printing office since in the last pages the supply of *'s and †'s ran out and other characters were substituted. Many Dens used only this Prescript, and most of the members have never heard of more than one Prescript.

In some respects this first Constitution was found defective and in 1868 the Revised and Amended Prescript was adopted. Who framed it we do not know, but it is known how it was printed. Frank O. McCord, one of the founders of the Pulaski Circle, was editor of the *Pulaski Citizen*. A relative of his who worked in the printing office of the *Citizen,* made the following statement some years ago in reference to a copy of the Revised and Amended Prescript.[1]

---

[1] It is the copy he refers to that is reproduced in Appendix II.

"This is an exact copy of the original Prescript printed in the office of the Pulaski (Tennessee) *Citizen,* L. W. McCord, proprietor, in 1868. I was a printer boy, and with John H. Kirk, the father of the Rev. Harry Kirk, recently of Nashville, set the type. My brother, L. W. McCord, received a communication one day, delivered to him by means of a hole in the wall near the door, in which the Ku Klux deposited all their communications for the paper, asking for an estimate for printing this pamphlet, describing it. He delivered his reply in the same hole, and the following morning the copy in full, the money, and minute directions as to the disposition of the books when completed, were in the hole. We did it all under seal of secrecy and concealment, hid the galleys of type as they were set up, stitched them with our own hands in a back room over Shapard's store, and trimmed them with a shoe knife on the floor. When finished they were tied into a bundle and deposited late at night just outside the office door, whence they were immediately taken by unseen hands. I knew personally all the originators of the Ku Klux Klan, and the history of its origin, its deeds, purposes and accomplishments.

"LAPS D. McCORD." [1]

It will be noticed on comparing the two Prescripts that there are some considerable differences between the two. The Revised and Amended Prescript is eight pages longer than the other; the name of the order is longer; the poetical selections that introduce the first are omitted from the second; the second has Latin quotations only at the top of the page; and the second Prescript throws much more light on the character and objects of the order; the register is changed, and important changes in the administration are provided for.

The imperfect Prescript printed in Appendix III was used in the Carolinas and was evidently written out from memory by some person who had belonged to the genuine Klan. The members were widely scattered and to many of them the entire contents of the Prescript were never known.

When the Klan was disbanded strict orders were issued that all documents

---

[1] *American Historical Magazine,* Vol. 5, p. 4.

relating to the order should be destroyed and few Prescripts escaped. At present only one copy of the original copy is known to be in existence. That one was used by Ryland Randolph, of Tuscaloosa, Alabama, formerly Grand Giant of a province of the order, and was given to me by him. It is a little brown pamphlet of sixteen pages, and is reprinted in Appendix I. Randolph stated that he never saw the Revised Prescript. There are two copies of the Revised and Amended Prescript, one in the library of the Southern Society of New York, which is now deposited with the Columbia University Library; the other belongs to Mr. J. L. Pearcy, formerly of Nashville, now of Washington, D. C. From the latter copy the late Dr. W. R. Garrett, of Nashville, had the plates made that are now used in reproducing the Revised and Amended Prescript in Appendix II.

The curious orders and warnings printed in Appendix IV had several purposes. They were meant to warn and frighten evil-doers, to mystify the public, and to give notice to members. Parts of the orders were written in cypher which could be interpreted by the initiated. The rest

was gloomy sounding nonsense calculated
to alarm some obnoxious person or persons. The cypher used is found in the
Register of the Prescript. All orders that
I have seen were written according to the
Register of the first Prescript. This may
be accounted for by the fact that in 1868 it
was generally forbidden by law or by military order to print or distribute notices
from the Ku Klux Klan. About all that
the cypher was used for, I have been told,
was to fix dates, etc. There are thirty-one
adjectives in the Register, one for each day
of the month, the first twelve for the morning hours, the last twelve for the evening
hours, and the seven in the middle for the
days of the week. The last word—"Cumberland"—is said to have been a general
password. At first the orders were printed in the newspapers, and during the winter of 1867-1868 and the spring of 1868
many of them appeared. As to the significance of the orders printed in Appendix
IV, Ryland Randolph wrote: "I well remember those notices you saw in *The
Monitor* for they were concocted and posted by my own hand, disguised, of course."
. . . . "You ask if any of the
notices you saw in *The Monitor* had any

real meaning. Well, they had this much
meaning: the very night of the day on
which these notices made their appearances, three notably offensive negro men
were dragged out of their beds, escorted to
the old bone-yard (¾ mile from Tuscaloosa) and thrashed in the regular ante-bel-
lum style until their .unnatural nigger
pride had a tumble, and humbleness to the
white man reigned supreme."

Some of the illustrations used are of his-
torical interest. The cartoon opposite p. 192
is taken from the *Independent Monitor* of
Tuscaloosa, Alabama, a Ku Klux newspaper. The hanging carpetbagger was
Rev. A. S. Lakin, of Ohio, a Northern
Methodist missionary to the negroes, who
had succeeded in getting himself elected
President of the University of Alabama.
The other hanging figure represents Dr.
N. B. Cloud, the scalawag superintendent
of public instruction who was assisting
Lakin to get his position. They were both
driven from Tuscaloosa by the Klan. The
wood-cut from which this picture was
printed was fashioned by Randolph himself in *The Monitor* office. The picture was
eagerly welcomed by the Reconstruction-

ists as an evidence of the state of affairs in Alabama, and it was reproduced far and wide during the Presidential campaign of 1868. Randolph's brother Democrats were furious because he had furnished such excellent campaign material to the other side. In one of Randolph's letters he states: "The name of the Ohio newspaper that republished my famous wood-cut was the *Cincinnati Commercial*. I have good authority for stating that said paper issued 500,000 copies for distribution throughout Ohio during the Seymour-Grant campaign. Not only this, but a Columbus, Ohio, paper also issued a large edition."

The cartoon opposite p. 113 is reproduced from "The Loil Legislature," a pamphlet by Capt. B. H. Screws, of Montgomery. The Alabama Reconstruction Legislature was the first to make an investigation of Ku Klux Klan and *Sibley* and *Coon* were two carpetbaggers active in the investigation.

Opposite p. 196 is a typical warning sent to persons obnoxious to the Klan. It is taken from the Ku Klux Report, Alabama Testimony.

The costumes represented opposite p. 58 were captured in Mississippi and were

worn both in Mississippi and in Western
Alabama. The costumes represented opposite p. 97 were captured after the famous
Ku Klux parade in Huntsville, Alabama,
in 1868.   Federal soldiers donned the captured disguises and were photographed.
During the campaign of 1868 the pictures
were reproduced in the Reconstructionist
newspapers.

Miss Cora R. Jones kindly furnished a
drawing (see outside cover) of the badge
worn by the higher officials of the Klan,
and a sketch of the room (see p. 53) in
which the Klan was founded.   Her uncle,
Calvin Jones, was one of the founders, the
father, Charles P. Jones, was also a member and the badge mentioned belonged to
him.

The text of the Lester and Wilson History is reprinted without change.

West Virginia University,

   October, 1905.

KU KLUX KLAN

ITS ORIGIN, GROWTH AND DISBANDMENT

BY

J. C. LESTER AND D. L. WILSON

KU KLUX KLAN

CHAPTER I.

THE ORIGIN.

THERE is no stranger chapter in American history than the one which bears for a title "Ku Klux Klan." The organization which bore this name went out of life as it came into it, shrouded in deepest mystery. Its members would not disclose its secrets; others could not. Even the investigation committee, appointed by Congress, were baffled. The voluminous reports containing the results of that committee's tedious and diligent inquiry do not tell when and where and how the Ku Klux Klan originated. The veil of secrecy still hangs over its grave. We propose to lift it.

The time has now arrived when the history of the origin, growth and final decay of "The Invisible Empire" may be given

to the public.   Circumstances not necessary to detail have put it in the power of
the writer to compile such a history.   For
obvious reasons the names of individuals
are withheld.   But the reader may feel
assured that this narrative is drawn from
sources which are accurate and authentic.

The writer does not profess to be able
to disclose the secret signs, grips and pass-
words of the order.[1]   These have never
been disclosed and probably never will be.
But we claim to narrate facts relating to
the order, which have a historic and phil-
osophic value.   It is due to the truth of
history; to the student of human nature;
to the statesmen, and to the men who
were engaged in this movement, that the
facts connected with this remarkable epi-
sode in our nation's history be frankly and
fairly told.

A wave of excitement, spreading by
contagions till the minds of a whole people are in a ferment, is an event of frequent occurrent.   The Ku Klux movement was peculiar by reason of the causes

---

[1] The writer, D. L. Wilson, was not a member.
The secrets of the Klan were not printed or written, but were communicated orally.   In Appendix
IV, p. 197, will be found versions of the oath taken
by the members.—*Editor.*

which produced and fed the excitement.
It illustrates the weird and irresistible
power of the unknown and mysterious
over the minds of men of all classes and
conditions in life. And it illustrates how
men, by circumstances and conditions, in
part of their own creation, may be carried
away from their moorings and drifted
along in a course against which reason
and judgment protest.

The popular idea supposes the Ku Klux
movement to have been conceived in
malice, and nursed by prejudice and hate,
for lawlessness, rapine and murder. The
circumstances which brought the Klan
into notice and notoriety were of a character to favor such conclusions. No other
seemed possible. The report of the Congressional Investigating Committee confirmed it.[1] Even if that report be true,
like everything else which is known of the
Ku Klux, it is fragmentary truth. The
whole story has never been told. And the

---

[1] In 1871-1872 a Committee of Congress made an
investigation of affairs in the South. Its report,
with the testimony collected, was published in 13
volumes, and is usually called the Ku Klux Report.
See Fleming, Civil War and Reconstruction in Alabama, p. 701; Garner, Reconstruction in Mississippi, p. 344.—*Editor.*

impression prevails that the Ku Klux
Klan was conceived and carried out in
pure and unmixed deviltry. The reader
who follows this narrative to its end will
decide, with the facts before him, whether
this impression is just and true.

The Ku Klux Klan was the outgrowth
of peculiar conditions, social, civil and
political, which prevailed at the South
from 1865 to 1869. It was as much a prod-
uct of those conditions as malaria is of a
swamp and sun heat.

Its birthplace was Pulaski, the capital
of Giles, one of the southern tier of counties in Middle Tennessee. Pulaski is a
town of about three thousand inhabitants.
Previous to the war its citizens possessed
wealth and culture—they retain the second—the first was lost in the general
wreck. The most intimate association
with them fails to disclose a trace of the
diabolism which, according to the popular
idea, one would expect to find character-
izing the people among whom the Ku
Klux Klan originated. A male college and
a female seminary are located at Pulaski,
and receive liberal patronage. It is a town
of churches.

There, in 1866, the name Ku Klux first fell from human lips. There began a movement which in a short time spread as far north as Virginia[1] and as far south as Texas, and which for a period convulsed the country and attracted the attention of the civilized world. Proclamations were fulminated against the Klan by the President and by the Governors of States; and hostile statutes were enacted both by State and National Legislatures.

It was finally quieted, but not until there had become associated with the name Ku Klux gross mistakes and lawless deeds of violence. To this day there are localities where the utterance of it awakens awe and fear.

During the entire period of the Klan's organized existence, Pulaski continued to be its central seat of authority. Some of its highest officers resided there. This narrative, therefore, will relate principally to the growth of the Klan and the measures taken to suppress it in Tennessee. It is necessary to a clear understanding of the movement to observe that the history of the Klan is marked by two distinct and well defined periods. The first period

---

[1] See above, p. 23.

covers the time from its organization, in
1866, to the summer of 1867. The second
from the summer of 1867 to the date of its
disbandment in the early part of the year
1869.[1]

The first period contains but little of
general interest, but it is necessary to describe it somewhat minutely, because of
its bearing on subsequent events. When
the war ended, the young men of Pulaski,
who had escaped death on the battlefield,
returned home and passed through a
period of enforced inactivity. In some
respects it was more trying than the
ordeal of war which lay behind them. The
reaction which followed the excitement of
army scenes and service was intense.
There was nothing to relieve it. They
could not engage at once in business or
professional pursuits. In the case of
many, business habits were broken up.
Few had capital to enter mercantile or
agricultural enterprises. There was a
total lack of the amusements and social
diversions which prevail wherever society
is in a normal condition.

---

[1] General Forrest said that the order was disbanded in the fall of 1868. See Ku Klux Report,
Vol. XIII., pp. 3-35.—*Editor.*

ROOM IN WHICH THE KLAN WAS FOUNDED

Law office of Judge Thomas M. Jones, Pulaski, Tennessee.   From sketch by Miss Cora R. Jones

One evening in May, 1866,[1] a few of these young men met in the office of one of the most prominent members of the Pulaski bar. [2] In the course of the conversation one of the number said: "Boys, let us get up a club or society, of some description." The suggestion was discussed with enthusiasm. Before they separated it was agreed to invite others, whose names were mentioned, to join them, and to meet again the next evening at the same place. At the appointed time eight or[3] ten young men had assembled.

A temporary organization was effected by the election of a chairman and a secretary. There was entire unanimity among the members in regard to the end in view, which was diversion and amusement. The evening was spent in discussing the best means of attaining the object for which they were seeking. Two committees were appointed, one to select a name,[4] the

---

[1] Wilson's account in the *Century Magazine,* July, 1884, says that the order was founded in June, 1866.—*Editor.*

[2] This was the law office of Judge Thomas M. Jones, father of one of the originators.—*Editor.*

[3] Survivors say that six men organized the club and that others joined soon after.—*Editor.*

This committee was composed of Calvin Jones and R. R. Reed.—*Editor.*

other[1] to prepare a set of rules for the government of the society, and a ritual for the initiation of new members. The club adjourned to meet the following week to hear and act upon the reports of these committees. Before the arrival of the appointed time for the next meeting, one of the wealthiest and most prominent citizens of Pulaski went on a business trip to Columbus, Miss., taking his family with him. Before leaving he invited one of the leading spirits of the new society to take charge of and sleep at his house during his absence. This young man invited his comrades to join him there. And so the place of meeting was changed from the law office to this residence. The owner of it outlived the Ku Klux Klan and died ignorant of the fact that his house was the place where its organization was fully effected.

This residence afterwards came into the possession of Judge H. M. Spofford, of Spofford-Kellogg fame.[2] It was his

---

[1] In this committee were J. R. Crowe, J. C. Lester and John Kennedy.—*Editor*.

[2] Spofford was a brother of A. R. Spofford, Librarian of Congress. He was a native of New Hampshire, who removed to Louisiana and held

home at the time of his death, and is still owned by his widow.

The committee appointed to select a name reported that they had found the task difficult, and had not made a selection. They explained that they had been trying to discover or invent a name which would be, to some extent, suggestive of the character and objects of the society. They mentioned several which they had been considering. In this number was the name "Kukloi" from the Greek word *Kuklos* (Kuklos), meaning a band or circle. At mention of this some one cried out: "Call it Ku Klux." "Klan" at once suggested itself, and was added to complete the alliteration. So instead of adopting a name, as was the first intention, which had a definite meaning, they chose one which to the proposer of it, and to every one else, was absolutely meaningless.

This trivial and apparently accidental incident had a most important bearing on

high judicial office there before the Civil War. After 1870 he spent much of his time in Pulaski. In 1877 he was elected to the United States Senate from Louisiana, but the Senate seated W. P. Kellogg, a carpetbagger from Illinois, who had been voted for by the "Packard Legislature." —*Editor.*

the future of the organization so singular-
ly named. Looking back over the history
of the Klan, and at the causes under which
it developed, it is difficult to resist the conclusion that the order would never have
grown to the proportions which it afterwards assumed, or wielded the power it
did, had it not borne this name or some
other equally as meaningless and mysterious—mysterious because meaningless.

Had they called themselves the "Jolly
Jokers" or the "Adelphi," or by some similar appellation, the organization would
doubtless have had no more than the mere
local and ephemeral existence which those
who organized it contemplated for it.
Hundreds of societies have originated
just as this one did, and after a brief existence have passed away. But in this
case there was a weird potency in the very
name Ku Klux Klan. Let the reader pronounce it aloud. The sound of it is suggestive of bones rattling together! The
potency of the name was not wholly in the
impression made by it on the general public. It is a singular fact that the members
of the Klan were themselves the first to
feel its weird influence; they had adopted
a mysterious name. Thereupon the origi-

nal plan was modified so as to make everything connected with the order harmonize
with the name.

Amusement was still the end in view.
But now the method by which they propose to win it were those of secrecy and
mystery. So when the report of the committee on rules and ritual came up for consideration, the recommendations were
modified to adapt them to the new idea.
The report as finally adopted, provided
for the following officers: a Grand Cyclops, or President; a Grand Magi, or
Vice-President; a Grand Turk, or Mar-
shal; a Grand Exchequer, or Treasurer;
and two Lictors. These were the outer
and inner guards of the "Den," as the
place of meeting was designated.

The one obligation exacted from members was to maintain profound and abso-
lute secrecy with reference to the order and
everything pertaining to it. This obligation prohibited those who assumed it from
disclosing that they were Ku Klux, or the
name of any other member, and from so-
liciting any one to become a member. The
last requirement was a singular one. It
was enacted for two reasons. First, it
was in keeping with the determination to

appear as mysterious as possible, and thus play upon the curiosity of the public. Secondly, and mainly, it was designed to prevent unpleasantness following initiations. They wished to be able to say to novices: "You are here on your own solicitation, and not by invitation from us." They desired accessions; to have them was indispensable; but they knew human nature well enough to know that if they made the impression that they wished to be exclusive and select, then applications for membership would be numerous. The result showed that they reasoned correctly.

Each member was required to provide himself with the following outfit: A white mask for the face, with orifices for the eyes and nose; a tall, fantastic cardboard hat, so constructed as to increase the wearer's apparent height; a gown, or robe, of sufficient length to cover the entire person. No particular color or material were prescribed. These were left to the individual's taste and fancy, and each selected what in his judgment would be the most hideous and fantastic, with the aim of inspiring the greatest amount of curiosity in the novice. These robes, of different colors, often of the most flashy

Costumes Worn in Mississippi and West Alabama

patterns of "Dolly Varden" calicos, added vastly to the grotesque appearance of the assembled Klan.[1]

Each member carried also a small whistle, with which, by means of a code of signals agreed upon, they held communications with one another. The only utility of this device was to awaken inquiry.[2]

And the object of all this was amusement—"only this, and nothing more." A few young men debarred for the time by circumstances from entering any active business or professional pursuits, and deprived of the ordinary diversions of social life, were seeking in this way to amuse and employ themselves. The organization of this Klan was to them both diversion and occupation. But where, it may be asked, did the fun come in?

---

[1] "Their robes used in these nocturnal campaigns consisted simply of sheets wrapped around their bodies and belted around the waist. The lower portion reached to the heels, whilst the upper had eye-holes through which to see and mouth-holes through which to breathe. Of course, every man so caparisoned had one or more pistols in holsters buckled to his waist."—*Ryland Randolph.*

[2] It is said that the members of the Pulaski Den wore small metal badges.—*Editor.*

Partly in exciting the curiosity of the public, and then in baffling it; but mainly in the initiation of new members.

The ritual used in the initiation was elaborate, but not worthy of reproduction. It is enough to say that it was modeled on and embraced the leading features of the ritual of an order which has long been popular in colleges and universities under various names.[1] In one place it is the "Sons of Confucius;" in another, the "Guiasticutus;" but everywhere, the "Ancient and the Honorable," and the "Mirth-Provoking."

The initiations were at first conducted in the law office, where the suggestion for the formation of the Klan had been made. But it was not a suitable place. The room was small. It was near the business portion of the town, and while in session there, they never felt entirely free from apprehensions of interruption.[2]

---

[1] In the Southern colleges of today the peculiar Greek letter fraternity known as Alpha Sigma Sigma, and the institution of "snipe hunting" most nearly resemble the Klan in its early stages.— *Editor.*

[2] After leaving the law office of Judge Jones the Klan met for a while in a room of the *Pulaski Citizen* building. The editor of the *Citizen* was

They soon found a place in every respect better adapted to their purposes. On the brow of a ridge, that runs along the western outskirts of the town, there used to stand a handsome and commodious residence. The front, or main building, was of brick, the "L" of wood. In December, 1865, the brick portion of this house was demolished by a cyclone. The "L" remained standing, but tenantless. It consisted of three rooms. A stairway led from one of them to a large cellar beneath. No other house stood near. Around these ruins were the storm-torn, limbless trunks of trees, which had once formed a magnificent grove. Now, they stood up, grim and gaunt, like spectre sentinels. A dreary, desolate, uncanny place it was. But it was, in every way, most suitable for a "den," and the Klan appropriated it.[1]

When a meeting was held, one Lictor was stationed near the house, the other fifty yards from it on the road leading

---

a member of the Klan and his paper published the orders, proclamations and warnings sent out by the officials.—*Miss Cora R. Jones.*

[1] This building was the property of Dr. Benjamin Carter, grandfather of the present postmaster of Birmingham, Alabama.—*Miss Cora R. Jones.*

into town. These were dressed in the fantastic regalia of the order and bore tremendous spears as the badge of their office.

As before stated, and for the reasons assigned, the Ku Klux did not solicit any one to join them; yet, they had applications for membership. While members were not allowed to disclose the fact of their membership, they were permitted to talk with others in regard to anything that was a matter of common report with reference to the order. If they chose, members were allowed to say to outsiders: "I am going to join the Ku Klux." If the persons addressed expressed a desire to do likewise, the Ku Klux would say, if the party was a desirable one: "Well, I think I know how to get in. Meet me at such a place, on such a night, at such an hour, and we will join together." Other similar subterfuges were resorted to, to secure members without direct solicitation. Usually, curiosity would predominate over every other consideration, and the candidate would be found waiting at the appointed place.

As the Ku Klux and the candidate approached the sentinel Lictor, they were hailed and halted and questioned. Having received the assurance that they desired to become Ku Klux, the Lictor blew the signal for his companion to come and take charge of the novices. The candidate, under the impression that his companion was similarly treated, was blindfolded and led to the "den." The preliminaries of the initiation consisted in leading the candidate around the rooms and down into the cellar, now and then placing before him obstructions which added to his discomfort, if not to his mystification. After some rough sport of this description, he was led before the Grand Cyclops who solemnly addressed to him numerous questions. Some of these questions were grave, and occasionally a faulty answer resulted in the candidate's rejection. For the most part they were absurd to the last degree. If the answers were satisfactory, the obligation to secrecy, already administered, was exacted a second time. Then the Grand Cyclops commanded:

"Place him before the royal altar and adorn his head with the regal crown."

The "royal altar" was a large looking glass. The "regal crown" was a huge hat bedecked with two enormous donkey ears. In this headgear the candidate was placed before the mirror and directed to repeat the couplet:

> "O wad some power the giftie gie us
> To see oursel's as ithers see us."

As the last word was falling from his lips, the Grand Turk removed the bandage from his eyes, and before the candidate was his own ludicrous image in the mirror. To increase the discomfiture and chagrin which any man in such a situation would naturally feel, the removal of the bandage was the signal to the Klan for indulgence in the most uproarious and boisterous mirth. The Grand Cyclops relaxed the rigor of his rule, and the decorum hitherto maintained disappeared, and the "den" rang with shouts and peals of laughter; and worse than all, as he looked about him, he saw that he was surrounded by men dressed in hideous garb and masked, so that he could not recognize one of them.

The character of these initiatory proceedings explains why, from the very first, secrecy was so much insisted on. A single "tale out of school" would have spoiled the fun. For the same reason the Klan,

in its early history, was careful in regard
to the character of the men admitted. Rash
and imprudent men—such as could not be
confidently relied upon to respect their
obligation to secrecy—were excluded.
Nor were those admitted who were addic-
ted to the use of intoxicants. Later on in
the history they were not so careful, but in
the earlier period of its existence the Klan
was composed of men of good habits.[1]

In some instances, persons not regarded
as eligible to membership, or not desirable,
were persistent even to annoyance in their
efforts to gain admission to the order.
Such persistence was occasionally rebuked
in a manner more emphatic than tender.

One young man had a consuming desire
to be a Ku Klux. The sole objection to
him was his youth. When he presented
himself to the Lictor, the latter received
him kindly, and led him blindfold, "over
the hill and far away" to a secluded spot,

---

[1] "My information was that they admitted no
man who was not a gentleman and a man who
could be relied upon to act discreetly; not men
who were in the habit of drinking, boisterous men,
or men liable to commit error or wrong."—
*General Forrest in Ku Klux Report, Vol. XIII,
p. 22.*

and left him with the admonition to "wait there till called for." After hours of weary waiting, the young man removed the bandage from his eyes and sought the shelter of the paternal roof.

Another of riper years, but for some reason not acceptable to the order, made repeated efforts to join the Klan. For his special benefit they arranged to have an initiation not provided for in the ritual. A meeting was appointed to be held on the top of a hill that rises by a gentle slope to a considerable height, on the northern limits of Pulaski. The candidate, in the usual way—blindfold excepted—was led into the presence of the Grand Cyclops. This dignitary was standing on a stump. The tall hat, the flowing robe, and the elevated position made him appear not less than ten feet tall. He addressed to the candidate a few unimportant and absurd questions, and then, turning to the Lictors, said: "Blindfold the candidate and proceed."

The "procedure" in this case was to place the would-be Ku Klux in a barrel, provided for the purpose, and to send him whirling down the hill! To his credit, be it said, he never revealed any of the secrets of the Ku Klux Klan.[1]

These details have an important bearing on the subsequent history of the Ku Klux. They show that the originators of the Klan were not meditating treason or lawlessness in any form. Yet the Klan's later history grew naturally out of the measures and methods which characterized this period of it. Its projectors did not expect it to spread. They thought it would "have its little day and die." It lived; it grew to vast proportions.

---

[1] Later, when Brownlow's Administration was endeavoring to crush out the Ku Klux Klan, one of his detectives sought to gain admission to the order. His purposes became known and the Nashville Den, which he was trying to join, put him into a barrel and rolled it into the Cumberland River, drowning the detective.—*Washington Post, August* 13, 1905.

CHAPTER II.

THE SPREAD OF THE KLAN.

The devices for attracting attention were eminently successful. During the months of July and August, 1866, the Klan was much talked about by the citizens of Pulaski. Its mysteriousness was the sensation of the hour. Every issue of the local paper contained some notice of the strange order. These notices were copied into other papers, and in this manner the way was prepared for the rapid growth and spread of the Klan which soon followed.

Six weeks or less from the date of the organization the sensation in Pulaski had reached its height and was waning. Curiosity in regard to it had abated to such a degree that the Klan would have certainly fallen to pieces but for the following circumstances:

By the time the eligible material in the town had been used up, the young men from the country, whose curiosity had been inflamed by the newspaper notices, began to come in and apply for admission to the Klan. Some of these applications were accepted. In a little while the members from the country asked permission to establish "dens" at various points in the county. No provision had been made for such a contingency, but the permission was granted; had it not been, the result in all probability would have been the same.

As the ritual followed by the Pulaski Klan could not be conveniently carried out in the country, various modifications and changes were permitted. But the strictest injunctions were laid on these new lodges, or dens, in regard to secrecy, mystery and the character of the men admitted. The growth in the rural districts was more rapid than it had been in the town. Applications for permission to establish "dens" multiplied rapidly.

The news that the Ku Klux were spreading to the country excited the attention of the country people more generally than the existence of the Klan in town had done. The same cause rekindled the waning interest of the town people. Every issue of the local papers in the "infected regions" bristled with highly mysterious and exciting accounts of the doings of the "fantastic gentry."

During the fall and winter of 1866 the growth of the Klan was rapid. It spread over a wide extent of territory. Sometimes, by a sudden leap, it appeared in localities far distant from any existing "dens."

A stranger from West Tennessee, Mississippi, Alabama or Texas, visiting in a neighborhood where the order prevailed, would be initiated, and on his departure carry with him permission to establish a "den" at home. In fact, it was often done without such permission. The connecting link between these "dens" was very fragile. By a sort of tacit agreement the Pulaski Klan was regarded as the source of power and authority. The Grand Cyclops of this "den" was virtually the ruler of the order, but as he had no method of communicating with subjects or subordinates, and no way in which to enforce his mandates, his authority was more fancy than fact. But so far there had appeared no need for compact organization, rigid rules and close supervision. The leading spirits of the Ku Klux Klan

were contemplating nothing more serious
than amusement. They enjoyed the baffled curiosity and wild speculations of a
mystified public even more than the rude
sport afforded by the ludicrous initiations.

Such is the account of the Ku Klux
Klan in the first period of its history from
June, 1866, to April, 1867;[1] yet all this
time it was gradually, in a very natural
way, taking on new features not at first
remotely contemplated by the originators
of the order; features which finally transformed the Ku Klux Klan into a band of
"Regulators."

The transformation was effected by the
combined operation of several causes: (1)
The impressions made by the order upon
the minds of those who united with it;
(2) The impressions upon the public by
its weird and mysterious methods; (3)
The anomalous and peculiar condition of
affairs in the South at this time.

The mystery and secrecy with which
the Klan veiled itself made a singular
impression on the minds of many who
united with it.

---

[1] It will be remembered that in March, 1867,
the Reconstruction Acts were passed and that in
April, 1867, the Reconstruction was beginning.
—*Editor.*

The prevalent idea was that the Klan contemplated some great and important mission. This idea aided in its rapid growth. And on the other hand the rapid extensions of the Klan confirmed this idea of its purposes. When admitted to membership this conclusion, in the case of many, was deepened rather than removed by what they saw and heard. There was not a word in the ritual or in the obligation or in any part of the ceremony to favor such a conclusion; but the impression still remained that this mysteriousness and secrecy, the high-sounding titles of the officers, the grotesque dress of the members, and the formidable obligation, all meant more than real sport. This impression was ineradicable, and the attitude of many of the members continued to be that of expecting great developments. Each had his own speculations as to what was to be the character of the serious work which the Klan had to do. But they were satisfied that there was such work. It was an unhealthy and dangerous state of mind for men to be in; bad results in some cases very naturally followed from it.

The impression made by the Klan on the public was the second cause which contributed to its transformation into a band of Regulators. When the meetings first began to be held in the dilapidated house on the hill, passers-by were frequent. Most of them passed the grim and ghostly sentinel on the roadside in silence, but always with a quickened step. Occasionally one would stop and ask: "Who are you?" In awfully sepulchral tones the invariable answer was: "A spirit from the other world. I was killed at Chickamauga."

Such an answer, especially when given to a superstitious negro, was extremely terrifying, and if, in addition, he heard the uproarous noises issuing from the "den" at the moment of a candidate's investiture with the "regal crown," he had the foundation for a most awe-inspiring story. There came from the country similar stories. The belated laborer, passing after nightfall, some lonely and secluded spot, heard horrible noises and saw fearful sights. These stories were repeated with such embellishments as the imagination of the narrator suggested, till the feeling of the negroes and of many of the white people, at mention of the Ku Klux, was one of awe and terror.

In a short time the Lictor of the Pulaski "den" reported that travel along the road on which he had his post had almost entirely stopped. In the country it was noticed that the nocturnal perambulation of the colored population diminished, or entirely ceased, wherever the Ku Klux appeared. In many. ways there was a noticeable improvement in the habits of a large class who had hitherto been causing great annoyance. In this way the Klan gradually realized that the most powerful devices ever constructed for controlling the ignorant and superstitious were in their hands. Even the most highly cultured were not able wholly to resist the weird and peculiar feeling which pervaded every community where the Ku Klux appeared. Each week some new incident occurred to illustrate the amazing power of the unknown over the minds of men of all classes.

Circumstances made it evident that the measures and methods employed for sport might be effectually used to subserve the public welfare—to suppress lawlessness and protect property. When propositions to this effect began to be urged, there were many who hesitated, fearing danger.

The majority regarded such fears as groundless. They pointed to the good results which had already been produced. The argument was forcible—almost unanswerable. And the question was decided without formal action. The very force of circumstances had carried the Klan away from its original purpose. So that in the beginning of the summer of 1867 it was virtually, though not yet professedly, a band of regulators, honestly, but in an injudicious and dangerous way, trying to protect property and preserve peace and order.[1]

After all, the most powerful agency in effecting this transformation, the agency which supplied the conditions under which the two causes just mentioned became operative, was the peculiar state of affairs existing at the South at that time.

---

[1] "It originated with returned soldiers for the purpose of punishing those negroes who had become notoriously and offensively insolent to white people, and, in some cases, to chastise those white skinned men who, at that particular time, showed a disposition to affiliate socially with negroes. The impression sought to be made upon these latter was that these white-robed night prowlers were the ghosts of the Confederate dead, who had arisen from their graves in order to wreak vengeance on an undesirable class of both white and black men."—*Ryland Randolph.*

As every one knows, the condition of things was wholly anomalous, but no one can fully appreciate the circumstances by which the people of the South were surrounded except by personal observation and experience; and no one who is not fully acquainted with all the facts in the case is competent to pronounce a just judgment on their behavior. On this account, not only the Ku Klux, but the mass of the Southern people, have been tried, convicted and condemned at the bar of public opinion, and have been denied the equity of having the sentence modified by mitigating circumstances, which in justice, they have a right to plead.

At that time the throes of the great revolution were settling down to quiet. The almost universal disposition of the better class of the people was to accept the arbitrament which the sword had accorded them. On this point there was practical unanimity. Those who had opportunity and facilities to do so, engaged at once in agricultural, professional or business pursuits. There was but little disposition to take part in politics.

But there were two causes of vexation and exasperation which the people were in no good mood to bear. One of these causes related to that class of men who, like scum, had been thrown to the surface in the great upheaval.[1]

It was not simply that they were Union men from conviction. That would have been readily forgiven then, as can be shown by pointing to hundreds of cases. But the majority of the class referred to had played traitor to both sides, and were Union men now only because that was the successful side. And worse than all, they were now engaged in keeping alive discord and strife between the sections, as the only means of preventing themselves from sinking back into the obscurity from which they had been upheaved. Their conduct was malicious in the extreme and exceedingly exasperating. These men were a "thorn in the flesh" of the body, politic and social; and the effort to expel it set up an inflammation which for a time awakened the gravest apprehensions as to the result.

The second disturbing element was the negroes. Their transition from slavery to citizenship was sudden. They were

---

[1] The class called "tories" during the Civil War. They should not be confused with the genuine Unionists.—*Editor.*

not only not fitted for the cares of self-control, and maintenance so suddenly thrust upon them, but many of them entered their new role in life under the delusion that freedom meant license. They regarded themselves as freedmen, not only from bondage to former masters, but from the common and ordinary obligations of citizenship. Many of them looked upon obedience to the laws of the state—which had been framed by their former owners—as in some measure a compromise of the rights with which they had been invested. The administration of civil law was only partially re-established. On that account, and for other reasons, there was an amount of disorder and violence prevailing over the country which has never been equaled at any period of its history. If the officers of the law had had the disposition and ability to arrest all law-breakers, a jail and court-house in every civil district would have been required.

The depredations on property by theft and by wanton destruction for the gratification of petty revenge, were to the last degree annoying. A large part of these depredations was the work of bad white

men, who expected that their lawless
deeds would be credited to the negroes.
But perhaps the most potent of all causes
which brought about this transformation
was the existence in the South of a spu-
rious and perverted form of the "Union
League."[1]

It would be as unfair to this organization as it existed at the North, to charge
it with the outrages committed under
cover of its name, as it is to hold the Ku
Klux Klan responsible for all the lawlessness and violence with which it is
credited.

But it is a part of the history of those
times that there was a widespread and
desperately active organization called the
"Union League." It was composed of
the disorderly element of the negro
population and was led and controlled by
white men of the basest and meanest type
just now referred to. They met frequently, went armed to the teeth, and
literally "breathed out threatening and
slaughter." They not only uttered, but

---

[1] Sometimes called "Loyal League." See in
regard to this secret society—Fleming, Civil War
and Reconstruction in Alabama, Ch. 16, and
(West Virginia University) Documents relating
to Reconstruction, No. 3.—*Editor.*

in many instances executed the most violent threats against the persons, families and property of men, whose sole crime was that they had been in the Confederate army. It cannot be truthfully denied that the Ku Klux committed excesses and were charged with wrongdoing. But they were never guilty of the disorderly and unprovoked deeds of deviltry which mark the history of the Southern "Union League." It was partly, I may say chiefly, to resist this aggressive and belligerent organization that the Ku Klux transformed themselves into a protective organization.[1]

Whatever may be the judgment of history, those who know the facts will ever remain firm in the conviction that the Ku Klux Klan was of immense service at this period of Southern history. Without it, in many sections of the South, life to decent people would not have been tolerable. It served a good purpose. Wherever the Ku Klux appeared the

---

[1] On this point the testimony of Generals Forrest, John B. Gordon and E. W. Pettus, and J. A. Minnis, in the Ku Klux Report, is instructive. —*Editor*.

effect was salutary. For a while the robberies ceased. The lawless class assumed the habits of good behavior.

The "Union League" relaxed its desperate severity and became more moderate. Under their fear of the dreaded Ku Klux, the negroes made more progress, in a few months, in the needed lessons of self-control, industry, and respect for the rights of property and general good behavior, than they would have done in as many years, but for this or some equally powerful impulse.

It was a rough and a dangerous way to teach such lessons, but under all the circumstances it seemed the only possible way.

Of course, these men were trying a dangerous experiment. Many of them knew it at the time, and did not expect it on the whole to turn out more successfully than others of a similar character. But there seemed to be no other alternative at the time. Events soon occurred which showed that the fears of those who apprehended danger were not groundless, and it became evident, unless the Klan should be brought under better control than its leaders at this time exercised over it, that while it suppressed some evils, it would give rise to others almost, if not fully, as great.[1]

---

[1] Pease, "In the Wake of War," (fiction) gives a very good description of affairs in Tennessee by one who was thoroughly familiar with conditions there.

CHAPTER III.

THE TRANSFORMATION.

Until the beginning of the year 1867, the movements of the Klan had, in the main, been characterized by prudence and discretion; but there were some exceptions. In some cases there had been a liberal construction of orders and of what was by common consent the law of the Klan. In some, the limits, which tacitly it had been agreed upon not to pass, had been overstepped.

Attempts had been made to correct by positive means evils which menaces had not been sufficient to remove. Rash, imprudent and bad men had gotten into the order. The danger which the more prudent and thoughtful had apprehended as possible was now a reality. Had it been possible to do so, some of the leaders would have been in favor of disbanding. That could not well be done, because at that time the organization was so loose and imperfect. So to speak, the tie that bound them together was too shadowy to be cut or untied. They had evoked a spirit from "the vasty deep." It would not down at their bidding.

And, besides, the Klan was needed. The only course which seemed to promise any satisfactory solution of the difficulty was this: To reorganize the Klan on a plan corresponding to its size and present purposes; to bind the isolated dens together; to secure unity of purpose and concert of action; to hedge the members up by such limitations and regulations as were best adapted to restrain them within proper limits; to distribute the authority among prudent men at local centres, and exact from them a close supervision of those under their charge.

In this way it was hoped the impending dangers would be effectually guarded against. With these objects in view the Grand Cyclops of the Pulaski Den sent out a request to all the dens of which he had knowledge, to appoint delegates to meet in convention at Nashville, Tenn., in the early summer of 1867.[1] At the

---

[1] "In the spring of 1867," says Wilson in the *Century Magazine*, July, 1884. May was the month of meeting. This was just after the Reconstruction Acts had been passed.—*Editor.*

time appointed this convention was held. Delegates were present from Tennessee, Alabama, and a number of other States. A plan of reorganization, previously prepared, was submitted to this convention and adopted. After the transaction of some further business, the convention adjourned, and the delegates returned home without having attracted any attention.

At this convention the territory covered by the Klan was designated as the "Invisible Empire." This was subdivided into "realms" coterminous with the boundaries of States. The "realms" were divided into "dominions," corresponding to Congressional districts; the "dominions" into "provinces" coterminous with counties; and the "provinces" into "dens."

To each of these departments officers were assigned.

Except in the case of the supreme officer, the duties of each were minutely specified.

These officers were:

The Grand Wizard of the Invisible Empire and his ten Genii. The powers of this officer were almost autocratic.

The Grand Dragon of the Realm and his eight Hydras.

The Grand Titan of the Dominion and his six Furies.

The Grand Cyclops of the Den and his two Night Hawks.

A Grand Monk.

A Grand Scribe.

A Grand Exchequer.

A Grand Turk.

A Grand Sentinel.

The Genii, Hydras, Furies, Goblins and Night Hawks were staff officers. The gradation and distribution of authority was perfect. But for one source of weakness, the Klan, under this new organization, was one of the most perfectly organized orders that ever existed in the world.

As we shall see presently, it was vulnerable and failed because of the character of its methods. Secrecy was at first its strength. It afterwards became its greatest weakness. As long as mystery was conjoined with it, it was strength. When masks and disguises ceased to be mysterious, secrecy was weakness.

One of the most important things done by this Nashville convention was to make a positive and emphatic declaration of the principles of the order. It was in the following terms:

"We recognize our relations to the United States Government; the supremacy of the Constitution; the constitutional laws thereof; and the union of States thereunder."

If these men were plotting treason, it puzzles us to know why they should make such a statement as that in setting forth the principles of the order. The statement above quoted was not intended for general circulation and popular effect. So far as is known, it is now given to the public for the first time. We must regard it, therefore, as accurately describing the political attitude which the Ku Klux proposed and desired to maintain. Every man who became a member of the Klan really took an oath to support the Constitution of the United States.

This Nashville convention also defined and set forth the peculiar objects of the order, as follows:[1]

---

[1] I am convinced that the authors are mistaken in saying that the first convention adopted the Prescript containing these declarations. The Prescript adopted was the one reproduced in

(1.) "To protect the weak, the innocent, and the defenceless, from the indignities, wrongs and outrages of the lawless, the violent and the brutal; to relieve the injured and the oppressed; to succor the suffering, and especially the widows and orphans of Confederate soldiers.

(2.) "To protect and defend the Constitution of the United States, and all laws passed in conformity thereto, and to protect the States and people thereof from all invasion from any source whatever.

(3.) "To aid and assist in the execution of all constitutional laws, and to protect the people from unlawful seizure, and from trial except by their peers in conformity to the laws of the land."

This last clause was the result of the infamous and barbarous legislation of that day. On the 3rd of June, 1865, the Thirty-fourth General Assembly of Tennessee revived the sedition law and restricted the right of suffrage.[1] A negro

Appendix I. The other one, reproduced in Appendix II, was adopted, it is believed, in 1868.—*Editor.*

[1] Ex-Confederates were practically all excluded from the suffrage.—*Editor.*

militia, ignorant and brutal, were afterwards put over the State, and spread terror throughout its borders. Men felt that they had no security for life, liberty, or property. They were persecuted if they dared to complain. It was no strange thing if they resorted to desperate measures for protection. The emergency was desperate. Taking all the circumstances and aggravations into consideration one cannot but be surprised that men so persecuted and oppressed remained so moderate and forbearing.

The legislation of the Nashville Convention of Ku Klux bears internal evidence of what we know from other sources to be true. Whilst devising measures for protection to life and property, and for the resistance of lawlessness and oppression, whether from irresponsible parties or from those who professed to be acting legally and under cover of authority, they were anxious also to control the Klan itself and to keep it within what they conceived to be safe limits.

Up to this time the majority had shown a fair appreciation of the responsibilities of their self-imposed task of preserving social order. But under any circumstances the natural tendency of an organization such as this is to violence and crime—much more under such circumstances as those then prevailing.

Excesses had been committed. Whether justly so or not, they were credited to the Klan. And it was foreseen and feared that if such things continued or increased the hostility of State and Federal Governments would be kindled against the Klan and active measures taken to suppress it. The hope was entertained that the legislations taken by the convention and the reorganization would not only enable the Klan to enact its *role* as Regulators with greater success, but would keep its members within the prescribed limits, and so guard against the contingencies referred to. They desired on the one hand, to restrain and control their own members; on the other to correct evils and promote order in society; and to do the latter *solely* by utilizing for this purpose the means and methods originally employed for amusement. In each direction the success was but partial, as will be told presently.

By the reorganization no material change was made in the methods of the Klan's operations. Some of the old methods were slightly modified; a few new features were added. The essential features of mystery, secrecy and grotesqueness were retained, and steps were taken with a view to deepening and intensifying the impressions already made upon the public mind. They attempted to push to the extreme limits of illustration the power of the mysterious over the minds of men.

Henceforth they courted publicity as assiduously as they had formerly seemed to shun it. They appeared at different points at the same time, and always when and where they were the least expected. Devices were multiplied to deceive people in regard to their numbers and everything else, and to play upon the fears of the superstitious.

As it was now the policy of the Klan to appear in public, an order was issued by the Grand Dragon of the Realm of Tennessee to the Grand Giants of the Provinces for a general parade in the capital town of each Province on the night of the 4th of July, 1867. It will be sufficient for this narrative to describe that parade as witnessed by the citizens of Pulaski. Similar scenes were enacted at many other places.

On the morning of the 4th of July, 1867, the citizens of Pulaski found the sidewalks thickly strewn with slips of paper bearing the printed words:[1] "The Ku Klux will parade the streets to-night." This announcement created great excitement. The people supposed that their curiosity, so long baffled, would now be gratified. They were confident that this parade would at least afford them the opportunity to find out who were the Ku Klux.

Soon after nightfall the streets were lined with an expectant and excited throng of people. Many came from the surrounding country. The members of the Klan in the county left their homes in the afternoon and traveled alone or in squads of two or three, with their paraphernalia carefully concealed. If questioned, they answered that they were going to Pulaski to see the Ku Klux parade. After

---

[1] Notices were posted in every public place, and even pasted on the backs of hogs and cows running loose in the streets.—*Miss Cora R. Jones.*

nightfall they assembled at designated points near the four main roads leading into town. Here they donned their robes and disguises and put covers of gaudy materials on their horses. A skyrocket sent up from some point in the town was the signal to mount and move. The different companies met and passed each other on the public square in perfect silence; the discipline appeared to be admirable.[1] Not a word was spoken. Necessary orders were given by means of the whistles. In single file, in death-like stillness, with funeral slowness, they marched and counter-marched throughout the town. While the column was headed North on one street it was going South on another. By crossing over in opposite directions the lines were kept up in almost unbroken continuity. The effect was to create the impression of vast numbers. This marching and counter-marching was kept up for about two hours, and the Klan departed as noiselessly as they came. The public were more than ever mystified. Curiosity had not been satisfied, as it was

---

[1] Most members of the Klan had been Confederate soldiers and were familiar with military drill and discipline.—*Editor.*

expected it would be. The efforts of the most curious and cunning to find out who were Ku Klux failed. One gentleman from the country, a great lover of horses, who claimed to know every horse in the county, was confident that he would be able to identify the riders by the horses. With this purpose in view, he remained in town to witness fhe parade. But, as we have said, the horses were disguised as well as the riders. Determined not to be baffled, during a halt of the column he lifted the cove of a horse that was near him—the rider offering no objection—and recognized his own steed and saddle upon which he had ridden into town. The town people were on the alert also to see who of the young men of the town would be with the Ku Klux. All of them, almost without exception, were marked, mingling freely and conspicuously with the spectators. Those of them who were members of the Klan did not go into the parade.

This demonstration had the effect for which it was designed. Perhaps the greatest illusion produced by it was in regard to the numbers participating in it. Reputable citizens—men of cool and accurate judgment—were confident that the number was not less than three thousand. Others, whose imaginations were more easily wrought upon, were quite certain there were ten thousand. The truth is, that the number of Ku Klux in the parade did not exceed four hundred. This delusion in regard to numbers prevailed wherever the Ku Klux appeared. It illustrates how little the testimony of even an eye-witness is worth in regard to anything which makes a deep impression on him by reason of its mysteriousness.

The Klan had a large membership; it exerted a vast, terrifying and wholesome power; but its influence was never at any time dependent on, or proportioned to, its membership. It was in the mystery in which the comparatively few enshrouded themselves. Gen. Forrest, before the Investigating Committee, placed the number of Ku Klux in Tennessee at 40,000,[1] and in the entire South at 550,000. This was with him only a guessing estimate.[2] Care-

---

[1] A later estimate places the membership of Ku Klux Klan at 72,000 in Tennessee alone. —*Washington Post, August* 13, 1905.

[2] Forrest denied that he had made such an estimate. There were many other orders similar to Ku Klux Klan and the total membership was probably about half a million.—*Editor.*

ful investigation leads to the conclusion
that he overshoots the mark in both cases.
It is an error to suppose that the entire
male population of the South were Ku
Klux, or that even a majority of them
were privy to its secrets and in sympathy
with its extremest measures. To many of
them, perhaps to a majority, the Ku Klux
Klan was as vague, impersonal and mysterious as to the people of the North, or of
England. They did attribute to it great
good and to this day remember with grat-
itude the protection it afforded them in the
most trying and perilous period of their
history, when there was no other earthly
source to which to appeal.[1]

---

[1] It made the women feel safer. "And then
came the reign of martial law, and the Freedmen's
Bureau. Those dark days of the Reconstruction
period rapidly followed the horrors of civil war,
and the reign of the carpetbagger began, goading
the people to desperation. For their protection
the younger and more reckless men of the
community now formed a secret society, which
masqueraded at night in grotesque and grewsome
character called the Ku Klux Klan. Always
silent and mysterious, mounted on horses, they
swept noiselessly by in the darkness with gleaming
death's heads, skeletons and chains. It struck
terror into the heart of the evil-doer, while the
peaceful citizen knew a faithful patrol had guarded
his premises while he slept."—*Mrs. Stubbs, in
"Saunders' Early Settlers of Alabama,"* p. 31.

COSTUMES WORN IN TENNESSEE AND NORTH ALABAMA

One or two illustrations may here be given of the methods resorted to to play upon the superstitious fears of the negroes and others.[1] At the parade in Pulaski, while the procession was passing a corner on which a negro man was standing, a tall horseman in hideous garb turned aside from the line, dismounted, and stretched out his bridle rein toward the negro, as if he desired him to hold his horse. Not daring to refuse, the frightened African extended his hand to grasp the rein. As he did so, the Ku Klux took his own head from his shoulders and offered to place that also in the outstretched hand. The negro stood not upon the order of his going, but departed with a yell of terror. To this day he will tell you: "He done it, suah, boss. I seed him do it." The gown was fastened by a draw-string over the top of the wearer's head. Over this was worn an artificial skull made of a large gourd or of pasteboard. This with the hat could be readily removed, and the man would then appear to be headless.

[1] A practice not mentioned here was that of sending out the peculiar warnings and orders, specimens of which are printed in Appendix IV.—*Editor.*

Such tricks gave rise to the belief—still prevalent among the negroes—that the Ku Klux could take themselves all to pieces whenever they wanted to.

Some of the Ku Klux carried skeleton hands. These were made of bone or wood with a handle long enough to be held in the hand, which was concealed by the gown sleeve. The possessor of one of these was invariably of a friendly turn and offered to shake hands with all he met, with what effect may be readily imagined.

A trick of frequent perpetration in the country was for a horseman, spectral and ghostly looking, to stop before the cabin of some negro needing a wholesome impression and call for a bucket of water. If a dipper or gourd was brought it was declined, and the bucket full of water demanded. As if consumed by raging thirst the horseman grasped it and pressed it to his lips. He held it there till every drop of the water was poured into a gum or oiled sack concealed beneath the Ku Klux robe. Then the empty bucket was returned to the amazed negro with the remark: "That's good. It is the first drink of water I have had since I was killed at Shiloh." Then a few words of counsel as to future behavior made an impression not easily forgotten or likely to be disregarded.

Under ordinary circumstances such devices are unjustifiable. But in the peculiar state of things then existing they served a good purpose. It was not only better to deter the negroes from theft and other lawlessness in this way than to put them in the penitentiary; but it was the only way, at this time, by which they could be controlled. The jails would not contain them. The courts could not or would not try them. The policy of the Klan all the while was to deter men from wrongdoing. It was only in rare, exceptional cases, and these the most aggravated, that it undertook to punish. [1]

---

[1] "We had regular meetings about once a week, at which the conduct of certain offensive characters would be discussed, and if the majority voted to punish such it would be accordingly done on certain prescribed nights. Sometimes it was deemed necessary only to post notices of warning, which, in some cases, were sufficient to alarm the victims sufficiently to induce them to reform in their behavior."—*Ryland Randolph.*

CHAPTER IV.

THE DECLINE.

For a while after the reorganization of the Klan, those concerned for its welfare and right conduct congratulated themselves that all was now well. Closer organization and stricter official supervision had a restraining influence upon the members. Many things seemed to indicate that the future work of the Klan would be wholly good.

These hopes were rudely shattered. Ere long official supervision grew less rigid or was less regarded. The membership was steadily increasing. Among the new material added were some bad men who could not be—at least were not—controlled.

In the winter and spring of 1867 and 1868 many things were done by members, or professed members, of the Klan, which were the subject of universal regret and condemnation. In many ways the grave censure of those who had hitherto been friendly to it was evoked against the Klan, and occasion, long sought for, was given its enemies to petition the intervention of the government to suppress it. The end came rapidly. We must now trace the causes which wrought the decay and downfall of the "Invisible Empire."

In regard to the doings of the Ku Klux two extreme positions have been advocated. On the one hand, it is asserted that the Ku Klux committed no outrages. On the other, that they were the authors of all the depredations committed by masked and disguised men in the Southern States from 1865 to 1869. The truth lies between these two extremes. Great outrages were committed by bands of disguised men during those years of lawlessness and oppression. And the fact must be admitted that some of these outrages were committed, if not by the order and approbation of the Klan, at least by men who were members of it.[1]

The thoughtful reader will readily understand how this came about.

There was a cause which naturally and almost necessarily produced the result.

---

[1] See Major Crowe's statement on p. 22.

Men of the character of the majority of those who composed the Klan do not disregard their own professed principles and violate self-assumed obligations without cause. We have seen that the Klan was in the main composed of the very best men in the country—peaceable, law-loving and law-abiding men—men of good habits and character—men of property and intelligence.

We have seen that the organization had no political significance; they expressly and in solemn secret compact declared their allegiance to the constitution and all constitutional laws, and pledged themselves to aid in the administration of all such laws. To see such men defying law and creating disorder, is a sight singular enough to awake inquiry as to the causes which had been at work upon them. The transformation of the Ku Klux Klan, from a band of regulators, honestly trying to preserve peace and order, into the body of desperate men who, in 1869, convulsed the country and set at defiance the mandates of both State and Federal governments, is greater than the transformation which we have already traced.

In both cases there were causes at work adequate to the results produced; causes from which, as remarked before, the results followed naturally and necessarily.

These have never been fully and fairly stated. They may be classed under three general heads: (1). Unjust charges. (2). Misapprehension of the nature and objects of the order on the part of those not members of it. (3). Unwise and over-severe legislation.

As has already been pointed out, the order contained within itself, by reason of the methods practiced, sources of weakness. The devices and disguises by which the Klan deceived outsiders enabled all who were so disposed, even its own members, to practice deception on the Klan itself. It placed in the hands of its own members the facility to do deeds of violence for the gratification of personal feeling, and have them credited to the Klan. To evilly-disposed men membership in the Klan was an inducement to wrongdoing. It presented to all men a dangerous temptation, which, in certain contingencies at any time likely to arise, it required a considerable amount of moral robustness to resist. Many did not withstand it. And deeds of violence were done by men who were Ku Klux, but who, while acting under cover of their connection with the Klan, were not under its orders. But because these men were Ku Klux, the Klan had to bear the odium of wrongdoing.[1]

In addition to this, the very class which the Klan proposed to hold in check and awe into good behavior, soon became wholly unmanageable. Those who had formerly committed depredations to be laid to the charge of the negroes, after a brief interval of good behavior, assumed

---

[1] "At this late day (1901) I am gratified to be able to say that my company did much good service to Tuscaloosa county. Had these organizations confined their operations to their legitimate object, viz: Punishing impudent negroes and negro-loving whites, then their performances would have effected only good. Unfortunately, the Klan began to degenerate into a vile means of wreaking revenge for personal dislikes or personal animosities, and in this way many outrages were perpetrated, ultimately resulting in casting so much well-deserved odium on the whole concern that about the year 1870 there was almost a universal collapse; all the good and brave men abandoning it in disgust. Many outrages were committed in the name of Ku Klux that really were done by irresponsible parties who never belonged to the Klan."—*Ryland Randolph.*

the guise of Ku Klux and returned to their old ways, but with less boldness and more caution, showing the salutary impression which the Klan had made upon them. In some cases the negroes played Ku Klux. Outrages were committed by masked men in regions far remote from any Ku Klux organizations. The parties engaged took pains to assert that they were Ku Klux, *which the members of the Klan never did.* This was evidence that these parties were simply aping Ku Klux disguises. The proof on this point is ample and clear. After the passage of the Anti Ku Klux Statute by the State of Tennessee, several instances occurred of parties being arrested in Ku Klux disguises; but in every instance they proved to be either negroes or "radical" Brownlow Republicans. This occurred so often that the statute was allowed by the party in power to become a dead letter before its repeal. It bore too hard on "loyal" men when enforced.

The same thing occurred in Georgia and other States. (See testimony of General Gordon and others before the Investigating Committee.)

No single instance occurred of the arrest of a masked man who proved to be—when stripped of his disguises—a Ku Klux.

But it came to pass that all the disorder done in the country was charged upon the Ku Klux, because done under disguises which they had invented and used. The Klan had no way in which to disprove or refute the charges. They felt that it was hard to be charged with violence of which they were innocent. At the same time they felt that it was natural, and, under the circumstances, not wholly unjust that this should be the case. They had assumed the office of Regulators. It was therefore due society, due themselves, and due the Government, which, so far, had not molested them, that they should, at least, not afford the lawless classes facilities for the commission of excesses greater than any they had hitherto indulged in, and above all, that they should restrain their own members from lawlessness.

The Klan felt all this; and in its efforts to relieve itself of the stigma thus incurred, it acted in some cases against the offending parties with a severity well merited, no doubt, but unjustifiable.[1] As is frequently the case they were carried beyond the limits of prudence and right by a hot zeal for self-vindication against unjust aspersions.

They felt that the charge of wrong was unfairly brought against them. To clear themselves of the charge they did worse wrong than that alleged against them.

The Klan from the first shrouded itself in deepest mystery; out of this fact grew trouble not at first apprehended. They wished people not to understand. They tried to keep them profoundly ignorant. The result was that the Klan and its objects were wholly misunderstood and misinterpreted. Many who joined the Klan and many who did not, were certain it contemplated something far more important than its overt acts gave evidence of. Some were sure it meant treason and revolution. The negroes and the whites whose consciences made them the subjects of guilty fears, were sure it boded no good to them.

---

[1] I have been told that in Tennessee several members of the Klan were executed by its orders for committing evil deeds under name of the Klan. —*Editor.*

When the first impressions of awe and terror which the Klan had inspired, to some extent, wore off a feeling of intense hostility towards the Ku Klux followed. This feeling was the more bitter because founded, not on overt acts which the Ku Klux had done, but on vague fears and surmises as to what they intended to do. Those who entertained such fears were in some cases impelled by them to become the aggressors. They attacked the Ku Klux before receiving from them any provocation. The negroes formed organizations of a military character and drilled by night, and even appeared in the day armed and threatening. The avowed purpose of these organizations was "to make war upon and exterminate the Ku Klux." On several occasions the Klan was fired into. The effect of such attacks was to provoke counter hostility from the Klan, and so there was irritation and counter-irritation, till, in some places, the state of things was little short of open warfare. In some respects it was worse; the parties wholly misunderstood each other. Each party felt that its cause was the just one. Each justified its deed by the provocation.

The Ku Klux, intending wrong, as they believed, to no one, were aggrieved that acts which they had not done should be charged to them; and motives which they did not entertain imputed to them and outraged that they should be molested and assaulted. The other party satisfied that they were acting in self-defense felt fully justified in assaulting them, and so each goaded the other on from one degree of exasperation to another.

The following extracts from a general order of the Grand Dragon of the Realm of Tennessee will illustrate the operation of both these causes. It was issued in the fall of the year 1868. It shows what were the principles and objects which the Klan still professed, and it also shows how it was being forced away from them:

HEADQUARTERS REALM No. 1, \
DREADFUL ERA, BLACK EPOCH, }
DREADFUL HOUR. /

General Order No. 1.

WHEREAS, Information of an authentic character has reached these headquarters that the blacks in the counties of Marshall, Maury, Giles and Lawrence are organized into military companies, with the avowed purpose to make war upon and exterminate the Ku Klux Klan, said blacks are hereby solemnly warned and ordered to desist from further action in such organizations, if they exist.

The G. D. [Grand Dragon] regrets the necessity of such an order. But this Klan shall not be outraged and interfered with by lawless negroes and meaner white men, who do not and never have understood our purposes.

In the first place this Klan is not an institution of violence, lawlessness and cruelty; it is not lawless; it is not aggressive; it is not military; it is not revolutionary.

It is, essentially, originally and inherently a protective organization. It proposes to execute law instead of resisting it; and to protect all good men, whether white or black, from the outrages and atrocities of bad men of both colors, who have been for the past three years a terror to society, and an injury to us all.

The blacks seem to be impressed with the belief that this Klan is especially their enemy. We are not the enemy of the blacks, as long as they behave themselves, make no threats upon us, and do not attack or interfere with us.

But if they make war upon us they must abide the awful retribution that will follow.

This Klan, while in its peaceful movements, and disturbing no one, has been fired into three times. This will not be endured any longer; and if it occurs again, and the parties be discovered, a remorseless vengeance will be wreaked upon them.

We reiterate that we are for peace and law and order. No man, white or black, shall be molested for his political sentiments. This Klan is not a political party; it is not a military party; it is a protective organization, and will never use violence except in resisting violence.

Outrages have been perpetrated by irresponsible parties in the name of this Klan. Should such parties be apprehended, they will be dealt with in a manner to insure us future exemption from such imposition. These impostors have, in some instances, whipped negroes. This is wrong! wrong! It is denounced by this Klan as it must be by all good and humane men.

The Klan now, as in the past, is prohibited from doing such things. We are striving to protect all good, peaceful, well-disposed and law-abiding men, whether white or black.

The G. D. deems this order due to the public, due to the Klan, and due to those who are misguided and misinformed. We, therefore, request that all newspapers who are friendly to law, and peace, and the public welfare, will publish the same.

By order of the G. D., Realm No. 1.

By the Grand Scribe.

This order doubtless expresses the principles which the Klan, as a body, was honestly trying to maintain. It also illustrates how they were driven to violate them by the very earnestness and vehemence with which they attempted to maintain them.

The question naturally arises, Why, under the embarrassing circumstances, did not the Klan disband and close its operations?[1] The answer is, that the members felt that there was now more reasons than ever for the Klan's existence. They felt that they ought not to abandon their important and needful work because they encountered unforeseen difficulties in accomplishing it. It is an illustration of the fatuity which sometimes marks the lives of men that they did not perceive what seems perfectly clear and plain to others. Nothing is more certain than that a part of the evils which the Klan was combating at this period of its history grew out of their own methods, and might be expected to continue as long as the Klan existed. Men are not always wise. But even in cases where their conduct does not permit of vindication and excuse, justice requires that a fair and truthful statement be made of the

---

[1] Some of the "Dens" disbanded in 1868. "As soon as our object was effected, viz., got the negroes to behave themselves, we disbanded."— *Ryland Randolph.*

CARPETBAGGERS LISTENING TO A KU KLUX REPORT

Coon and Sibly of the Alabama Legislature. Cartoon from Screw's
"Lost Legislature."

temptations and embarrassments which surrounded them. Placing all the circumstances before us fully, who of us is prepared to say that we would have acted with more wisdom and discretion than these men?

Matters grew worse and worse, till it was imperatively necessary that there should be interference on the part of the Government. In September, 1868, the Legislature of Tennessee, in obedience to the call of Governor Brownlow, assembled in extra session and passed a most stringent and bloody anti-Ku Klux statute.[1] This was the culmination of a long series of the most infamous legislations which ever disgraced a statute book.

It began in 1865, as we have seen, in the passage of the alien and sedition act, and grew worse and worse till the passage of the anti-Ku Klux statute in 1868. Sixteen years have passed since then, and many into whose hands this book will

---

[1] Most of the carpetbag and negro legislatures of the other Southern States passed similar laws, and Congress enacted a series of three "Force Laws" in 1870-1871. See Burgess' "Reconstruction and the Constitution," pp. 253, 262; Fleming's "Civil War and Reconstruction in Alabama," p. 695.—*Editor.*

come have never seen the "Anti-Ku Klux Law." We quote it entire, to show the character of the legislation of those times as well as for the sake of its bearing on the matter in hand:

Sec. 1. *Be it enacted, by the General Assembly of Tennessee,* That if any person or persons shall unite with, associate with, promote or encourage any secret organization of persons who shall prowl through the country or towns of this State, by day or by night, disguised or otherwise, for the purpose of disturbing the peace, or alarming the peaceable citizens of any portion of this State, on conviction by any tribunal of this State, shall be fined not less than five hundred dollars, imprisoned in the penitentiary not less than five years, and shall be rendered infamous.

Sec. 2. *Be it further enacted,* That it shall be the duty of all the courts in this State, before the impaneling of any grand jury or petit jury in any cause whatever, to inquire of the juror, on oath, whether he shall be associated in any way obnoxious to the first section of this act; and if such juror shall decline to give a voluntary answer, or shall answer affirmatively, such persons shall be disqualified as a juror in any case in any court in this State.

Sec. 3. *Be it further enacted,* That, for the purpose of facilitating the execution of the provisions of this act, it shall be the duty

of the Prosecuting Attorneys of this State
or grand jurors, or either of them, to summons or cause to be summoned, any persons
he shall have a well-grounded belief has any
knowledge of such organization as described
by the first section of this act, and if any
person shall fail or refuse to obey such summons, or shall appear and refuse to testify,
such persons so summoned shall suffer the
penalty imposed by the first section of this
act; and if such witness shall avoid the
service of said subpœna or summons, the
sheriff, or other officer, shall return such fact
on said process, when the court shall order
a copy of said process to be left at the last
place of residence of such persons sought to
be summoned; and if such person shall fail
to appear according to the command of said
process, said court shall enter a judgment
nisi against such person for the sum of five
hundred dollars, for which *sci. fa.* shall
issue, as in other cases of forfeiture of
subpœna.

SEC. 4. *Be it further enacted,* That no
prosecutor shall be required on any indictment under the provisions of this act; and
all the courts of the State shall give a
remedial construction to the same; and that
no presentment or indictment shall be
quashed, or declared insufficient for want
of form.

SEC. 5. *Be it further enacted,* That it
shall be the duty of all the courts of this
State, at every term, for two years from and
after the passage of this act, to call before

it all the officers thereof, who shall be sworn, and have this act read or explained to them; and the court shall ask said officers if they shall have any knowledge of any person of the State, or out of it, that shall be guilty of any of the offenses contained in this act, and that, if at any time they shall come to such knowledge, or shall have a well-grounded belief that any person or persons shall be guilty of a violation of this act or any of its provisions, that they will immediately inform the Prosecuting Attorney for the State thereof; and if such Prosecuting Attorney, upon being so informed, shall fail, refuse, or neglect to prosecute such person or persons so informed on, he shall be subject to the same penalties imposed by the first section of this act, and shall be stricken from the roll of attorneys in said court.

Sec. 6. *Be it further enacted,* That if any officer, or other person, shall inform any other person that he or she is to be summoned as a witness under any of the provisions of this act, or any other statute or law of this State, with the intent and for the purpose of defeating any of the provisions of this act, or any criminal law of this State; or if any officer, clerk, sheriff or constable shall refuse or fail to perform any of the duties imposed by this act, upon conviction, shall suffer the penalties by the first section of this act, and shall be disqualified from holding office in this State for two years.

SEC. 7. *Be it further enacted,* That if any person shall voluntarily inform on any person guilty of any of the provisions of this act, upon conviction such informant shall be entitled and receive one-half of the fine imposed; and if any officer, three-fourths.

SEC. 8. *Be it further enacted,* That if any person, guilty of any of the provisions or offenses enumerated in this act, that shall appear before any jury or prosecuting officer of the State, and shall inform him or them of any offense committed by any person or persons against the criminal laws of this State, such person or witness shall not be bound to answer to any charge for the violation of any provisions of any law about which such person or witness shall be examined; and the court shall protect such witness from any prosecution whatever.

SEC. 9. *Be it further enacted,* That where any process shall be issued against the person of any citizen in any county of this State, for any violation of the provisions of this act, and such shall be returned not executed, for any cause whatever, by the sheriff or other officer, to the court from which it was issued, with an affidavit appended thereto, plainly setting forth the reason for the non-execution of such process, then it shall be the duty of the clerk, without delay, to issue an *alias capias* to the same county, if the home of the defendant shall be in said county, either in part or in whole, when said sheriff or other officer shall give notice to

the inhabitants of said county by posting
such notice at the court-house of said county,
of the existence of said capias; and if the
inhabitants of such county shall permit such
defendant to be or to live in said county, in
part or in whole, the inhabitants shall be
subject to an assessment of not less than five
hundred dollars, nor more than five thousand
dollars, at the discretion of the court, which
said assessment shall be made in the following manner, to-wit: When the sheriff or
other officer shall return his *alias capias,*
showing that said defendant is an inhabitant
of said county, in part or in whole, and that
the citizens thereof have failed or refused to
arrest said defendant, which every citizen is
hereby authorized to do or perform. Said
court shall order *sci. fa.* to issue to the
proper officer to make known to the chairman, judge, or other presiding officer of the
County Court, to appear and show cause
why final judgment should not have been
entered up accordingly; which, if any
County Court fails or refuses to do and
perform, any judge, in vacation, shall grant
a *mandamus* to compel said County Court
to assess and collect said assessment, to be
paid into the State treasury for the benefit
of the school fund; provided, said assessment shall not be made of the sheriff or
other officer, upon the return of the original,
or *alias* writs, show cause why the same
cannot be executed, which may be done by
his affidavit and two respectable witnesses
known to the court as such.

SEC. 10. *Be it further enacted,* That all the inhabitants in this State shall be authorized to arrest any person defendant, under the provisions of this act, in any county in this State without process.

SEC. 11. *Be it further enacted,* That if any person or persons shall write, publish, advise, entreat or persuade, privately or publicly, any class of persons, or any individual, to resist any of the laws of this State calculated to molest or disturb the good people and peaceable citizens of the State, such persons shall be subject to the penalties of the first section of this act; and if an attorney at law, he shall be stricken from the roll of attorneys and be prevented from practicing in any court in this State.

SEC. 12. *Be it further enacted,* That if any person shall make threats against any elector or person authorized to exercise the elective franchise, with the intention of intimidating or preventing such person or persons from attending any election in this State, they shall be subject to the penalties inflicted by the first section of this act.

SEC. 13. *Be it further enacted,* That if any person or persons shall attempt to break up any election in this State, or advise the same to be done, with a view of preventing the lawful or qualified citizens of this State from voting, they shall be subject to the penalties prescribed by the first section of this act; and the attorney of the State in all convictions under the provisions of this act, shall be entitled to a tax fee of one hundred

dollars, to be taxed in the bill of costs, and
to be paid by the defendant. And the
attorney prosecuting for the State shall keep
all information given him a secret, unless it
shall be necessary, in the opinion of the
court, that the same should be made public.

Sec. 14. *Be it further enacted,* That it
shall be the duty of all the judges in this
State to read this act to the grand juries,
and give it especially in charge to said juries.

Sec. 15. *Be it further enacted,* That the
treasurer of this State shall not be authorized
to pay any judge in this State any salary,
or to any clerk, sheriff, or attorney, any fee
or bill of costs that may accrue to such
parties under the provisions of this act, until
such judge or other officer shall have filed
with the comptroller or treasurer an affidavit
plainly setting forth that he has fully com-
plied with the provisions of this act.

Sec. 16. *Be it further enacted,* That if
any person or citizen of this State shall
voluntarily feed, or lodge, or entertain, or
conceal in the woods, or elsewhere, any
offender known to such person to be charged
with any criminal offense under this act,
such person shall suffer the penalty prescribed by the first section of this act; provided, that this section shall not apply to
persons who, under the ancient law, might
feed or conceal the party charged.

Sec. 17. *Be it further enacted,* That if
any person, guilty of any of the offenses
enumerated in this act, shall have, own or
possess any real estate held by deed, or

grant, or entry, or by fee, or entail in law, or equity, the same shall be bound for costs, fines or penalties imposed by any of the provisions of this act; and a lien is hereby declared to attach to all estates in law or equity, as above, dating from the day or night of the commission of the offense, which fact may be found by the jury trying the cause, or any other jury impaneled for that purpose; and if in the opinion of the court the defendant has evaded the law, the jury shall find such fact, and the estate of the defendant shall be made liable for the costs of the State; and there shall be no limitation to the recovery of the same.

SEC. 18. *Be it further enacted,* That if any person or persons shall be guilty of a violation of any of the provisions of this act, to the prejudice or injury of any individual, the jury trying the defendant shall, or may find such fact with the amount of injury sustained, which shall be paid to the injured party or person entitled to the same, by the laws of descent of this State, with all costs, and who shall have the same lien on the property of the defendant that is possessed or given to the State by this act.

SEC. 19. *Be it further enacted,* That if any person shall knowingly make or cause to be made, any uniform or regalia, in part or in whole, by day or night, or shall be found in possession of the same, he, she or they shall be fined at the discretion of the court, and shall be rendered infamous.

SEC. 20. *Be it further enacted,* That in addition to the oath prescribed by the constitution and oath of office, every public officer shall swear that he has never been a member of the organization known as the Ku Klux Klan, or other disguised body of men contrary to the laws of the State, and that he has neither directly nor indirectly aided, encouraged, supported, or in any manner countenanced said organization.

SEC. 21. *Be it further enacted,* That the attorneys or prosecuting officers for the State, shall be entitled to and receive five per cent. on all forfeitures or assessments made by this act, on compensations to be paid by the defendant.

SEC. 22. *Be it further enacted,* That the standard of damages for injuries to individuals shall be as follows: For disturbing any of the officers of the State or other person, by entering the house or houses, or place of residence of any such individual in the night, in a hostile manner, or against his will, the sum of ten thousand dollars; and it shall be lawful for the person so assailed to kill the assailant. For killing any individual in the night twenty thousand dollars; provided, such person killed was peaceable at that time. That all other injuries shall be assessed by the court and jury in proportion; and the court trying said causes may grant as many new trials as may, in his opinion, be necessary to attain the end of justice.

SEC. 23. *Be it further enacted,* That all persons present, and not giving immediate information on the offenders, shall be regarded as guilty of a misdemeanor against the law, and shall be punished accordingly.

SEC. 24. *Be it further enacted,* That it shall not be lawful for any persons to publish any proffered or pretended order of said secret, unlawful clans; and any person convicted under any of the provisions of this act, shall not claim, hold, or possess any property, real or personal, exempt from execution, fine, penalty or costs, under this act; provided, that nothing herein contained shall be so construed as to prevent or exempt any person heretofore guilty of any of the offenses herein contained from prosecution under the law as it now stands. This act to take effect from after its passage.[1]

The same legislature passed a bill authorizing the Governor to organize, equip and call into active service, at his discretion, a volunteer force, to be known as the Tennessee State Guards; to be composed of one or more regiments from each congressional district of the State; provided always that said Tennessee State Guards shall be composed of loyal men.

---

[1] This is a good specimen of the "Force Laws" which were meant to uphold the Radical governments in the South against popular disaffection.— *Editor.*

And it was further provided by the "Militia Law," that upon the representation of "ten Union men, or three Justices of the Peace in any county in the State," that the presence of these troops were needed, that the Governor might declare martial law in such counties, and send thither troops in such numbers as, in his judgment, were necessary for the preservation of peace and order. And it was provided that the expense of these troops to the State should be collected from the counties where they were quartered.

The reader has now some insight into the character of the legislation direct against the Ku Klux. He will not only note the general severity and harshness of it, but the following features in particular:

(1). The anti-Ku Klux statute was *ex post facto,* as expressly declared by Section 24 of it. (2). It presented no way in which a man could relieve himself from liability to it, except by turning informer, and as an inducement to do this a large bribe was offered. (3). It encouraged strife, by making every inhabitant of the State an officer extraordinary with power "to arrest without process" when he had ground to suspect. (4). It must be remembered that in those days in Tennessee "to be loyal" had a very limited meaning. It meant simply to be a subservient tool and supporter of Governor Brownlow. If a man was not that, no matter what his past record, or what his political opinion, he was not "loyal." (5). While the law professed to be aimed at the suppression of all lawlessness, it was not so construed and enforced by the party in power. The "Union" or "Loyal" League was never molested, though this organization met frequently, and its members appeared by day and by night, armed, threatening and molesting the life and property of as peaceable and quiet citizens as any in the State. No attempt was ever made to arrest men except in Ku Klux disguises. But as before remarked there is no instance on record of a Ku Klux being arrested, tried and convicted. Invariably the party arrested while depredating as Ku Klux turned out to be, when stripped of their disguises, "loyal" men.

In some sections of the State a perfect reign of terror followed this anti-Ku Klux statute. The members of the Klan were now in the attitude of men fighting for life and liberty. Hundreds, perhaps thousands, of them were not lawbreakers, and did not desire to be. There had been no law against association with the Klan; they had conceived and done no wrong during their connection with it. They had had no participation in or knowledge of the excesses in which some of the Klan had indulged or were charged with having indulged in. But now their previous connection with the Klan was made a penal offense; and they had no hope except on terms which to men of honor and right principle were more odious than death.

These men were made infamous, made liable to fine and imprisonment, exposed to arrest without process by any malicious negro or mean white man; and even their wives and children were outlawed and exposed to the same indignities; and it is no strange thing if they were driven to the very verge of desperation. It is not denied that they did many things for which the world has been exceedingly slow to accept apology or excuse. But history is challenged to furnish an instance of a people bearing gross wrong and brutal outrage perpetrated in the name of law and loyalty with patience, forbearance or forgiveness, comparable to that exhibited by the people of the Southern States, and especially of Tennessee, during what is called the "Reconstruction period," and since.

There may be in their conduct some things to regret, and some to condemn; but he who gets a full understanding of their surroundings, social, civil and political, if he is not incapable of noble sentiment, will also find many things to awaken his sympathy and call forth his admiration.

CHAPTER V.

On the 20th day of February, 1869, Governor Brownlow resigned his position as Governor to take the seat in the United States Senate, to which he had been elected. The last paper to which he affixed his signature as Governor of Tennessee, proclaimed martial law in certain counties, and ordered troops to be sent thither. This proclamation was dated February 20, 1869. In a short while it was followed by a proclamation from the "Grand Wizard of the Invisible Empire" to his subjects.

This proclamation recited the legislation directed against the Klan, and stated that the order had now, in large measure, accomplished the objects of its existence. At a time when the civil law afforded inadequate protection to life and property, when robbery and lawlessness of every description were unrebuked, when all the better elements of society were in constant dread for the safety of their property, persons and families, the Klan had afforded protection and security to many firesides, and, in many ways contributed to the public welfare. But greatly to the regret of all good citizens, some members of the Klan had violated positive orders; others, under the name and disguises of the organization, had assumed to do acts of violence, for which the Klan was held responsible. The Grand Wizard had been invested with the power to determine questions of paramount importance to the interests of the order. Therefore, in the exercise of that power, the Grand Wizard declared that the organization heretofore known as the Ku Klux Klan was dissolved and disbanded.

Members were directed to burn all regalia and paraphernalia of every description, and to desist from any further assemblies or acts as Ku Klux.[1] The members of the Klan were counseled in the future as heretofore, to assist all good

---

[1] In the copy of the Revised and Amended Prescript owned by Columbia University Library is bound a letter in which is mentioned this order of destruction.—*Editor.*

people of the land in maintaining and upholding the civil laws, and in putting down lawlessness. This proclamation was directed to all Realms, Dominions, Provinces and "Dens" in "the Empire." It is reasonably certain that there were portions of the Empire never reached by it. The Klan was widely scattered and the facilities for communication exceedingly poor. The Grand Wizard was a citizen of Tennessee. Under the statute just now quoted newspapers were forbidden to publish anything emanating from the Klan. So that there was no way in which this proclamation could be generally disseminated.

Where it was promulgated, obedience to it was prompt and implicit. Whether obeyed or not, this proclamation terminated the Klan's organized existence as decisively and completely as General Lee's last general order, on the morning of the 10th of April, 1865, disbanded the army of Northern Virginia.

When the office of Grand Wizard was created and its duties defined, it was explicitly provided that he should have "the power to determine questions of paramount importance, and his decision shall be final." To continue the organization or to disband it was such a question. He decided in favor of disbanding, and so ordered. Therefore the Ku Klux Klan had no organized existence after March, 1869.[1]

The report of the Congressional Investigating Committee contains some disreputable history, which belongs to a later date, and is attributed to the Klan, but not justly so. For several years, after March, 1869, the papers reported and commented on "Ku Klux outrages" committed at various points. The authors of these outrages may have acted in the name of the Klan, and under its disguises; it may be that in some cases they were men who had been Ku Klux. But it cannot be charged that they were acting by the authority of an order which had formally disbanded. They were acting on their own responsibility.

Thus lived, so died, this strange order. Its birth was an accident; its growth was a comedy; its death a tragedy. It owed

---

[1] The local "Dens" were not affected by this order. Many had already disbanded; many more remained active as long as the Reconstruction régime lasted.—*Editor.*

its existence wholly to the anomalous condition of social and civil affairs in the South during the years immediately succeeding the unfortunate contest in which so many brave men in blue and gray fell, martyrs to their convictions.

There never was, before or since, a period of our history when such an order could have lived. May there never be again!

APPENDIX I.

PRESCRIPT OF KU KLUX KLAN

ADOPTED AT A CONVENTION OF THE ORDER
HELD IN NASHVILLE, APRIL, 1867

Copied from the Original Prescript, line for line and page for
page. The type used here is slightly larger than in
the original document.

Damnant quod non intelligunt   [1

PRESCRIPT
OF THE

*   *

What may this mean,
That thou, dead corse, again, in complete steel,
Revisit'st thus the glimpses of the moon,
Making night hideous; and we fools of nature,
So horridly to shake our disposition,
With thoughts beyond the reaches of our souls?

An' now auld Cloots, I ken ye're thinkin',
A certain *Ghoul* is rantin', drinkin',
Some luckless night will send him linkin',
          To your black pit;
But, faith! he'll turn a corner jinkin',
          And cheat you yet.

CREED.

We the * * reverently acknowledge the Majesty and Supremacy of the Divine being, and recognize the Goodness and Providence of the Same.

PREAMBLE.

We recognize our relations to the United States Government and acknowledge the supremacy of its laws.

APPELLATION.

ARTICLE I. This organization shall be styled and denominated the * *

TITLES.

ART. II. The officers of this * shall consist of a Grand Wizard of the Empire and his ten Genii; a Grand Dragon of the Realm and his eight Hydras; a Grand Titan of the Dominion and his six Furies; a Grand Giant of the Province and his four Goblins; a Grand Cyclops of the Den and his two Night Hawks; a Grand Magi, a Grand Monk, a Grand Exchequer, a Grand Turk, a Grand Scribe, a Grand Sentinel, and a Grand Ensign.

SEC. 2. The body politic of this * shall be designated and known as "Ghouls."

DIVISIONS.

ART. III. This * shall be divided into five departments, all combined, constituting the Grand * of the Empire. The second department to be called the Grand * of the Realm. The third, the Grand * of the Dominion. The fourth, the Grand * of the Province. The fifth, the * of the Den.

DUTIES OF OFFICERS.

GRAND WIZARD.

ART. IV. SEC. 1. It shall be the duty of the Grand Wizard, who is the Supreme Officer of the Empire, to communicate with and receive reports from the

Magna est veritas, et prevalebit.

Nec sci.·e fas est omnia.   [3

Grand Dragons of Realms, as to the condition, strength, efficiency and progress of the *s within their respective Realms. And he shall communicate from time to time, to all subordinates *s, through the Grand Dragon, the condition, strength, efficiency, and progress of the *s throughout his vast Empire; and such other information as he may deem expedient to impart. And it shall further be his duty to keep by his G Scribe a list of the names (without any caption or explanation whatever) of the Grand Dragons of the different Realms of his Empire, and shall number such Realms with the Arabic numerals, 1, 2, 3, &c., *ad finem*. And he shall instruct his Grand Exchequer as to the appropriation and disbursement which he shall make of the revenue of the * that comes to his hands. He shall have the sole power to issue copies of this Prescript, through his Subalterns and Deputies, for the organization and establishment of subordinate *s. And he shall have the further power to appoint his Genii; also, a Grand Scribe and a Grand Exchequer for his Department, and to appoint and ordain Special Deputy Grand Wizards to assist him in the more rapid and effectual dissemination and establishment of the * throughout his Empire. He is further empowered to appoint and instruct Deputies, to organize and control Realms, Dominions, Provinces, and Dens, until the same shall elect a Grand Dragon, a Grand Titan, a Grand Giant, and a Grand Cyclops, in the manner hereinafter provided. And when a question of paramount importance to the interest or prosperity of the * arises, not provided for in this Prescript, he shall have power to determine such question, and his decision shall be final, until the same shall be provided for by amendment as hereinafter provided.

Ne vile fano.

4]   Ars est celare artem

Grand Dragon.

Sec. 2. It shall be the duty of the Grand Dragon who is the Chief Officer of the Realm, to report to the Grand Wizard when required by that officer, the condition, strength, efficiency, and progress of the * within his Realm, and to transmit through the Grand Titan to the subordinate *s of his Realm, all information or intelligence conveyed to him by the Grand Wizard for that purpose, and all such other information or instruction as he may think will promote the interests of the *. He shall keep by his G. Scribe a list of the names (without any caption) of the Grand Titans of the different Dominions of his Realm, and shall report the same to the Grand Wizard when required; and shall number the Dominions of his Realm with the Arabic numerals, 1, 2, 3, &c., *ad finem*. He shall instruct his Grand Exchequer as to the appropriation and disbursement of the revenue of the * that comes to his hands. He shall have the power to appoint his Hydras; also, a Grand Scribe and a Grand Exchequer for his Department, and to appoint and ordain Special Deputy Grand Dragons to assist him in the more rapid and effectual dissemination and establishment of the * throughout his Realm. He is further empowered to appoint and instruct Deputies to organize and control Dominions, Provinces and Dens, until the same shall elect a Grand Titan, a Grand Giant, and Grand Cyclops, in the manner hereinafter provided.

Grand Titan.

Sec. 3. It shall be the duty of the Grand Titan who is the Chief Officer of the Dominion, to report to 'the Grand Dragon when required by that officer, the condition, strength, efficiency, and progress of the * within his Dominion, and to transmit through the Grand Giants to the subordinate *s

Nusquam tuta fides.

of his Dominion, all information or intelligence conveyed to him by the Grand Dragon for that purpose, and all such other information or instruction
as he may think will enhance the interests of the *.
He shall keep, by his G. Scribe, a list of the names
(without caption) of the Grand Giants of the different Provinces of his Dominion, and shall report the
same to the Grand Dragon when required; and he
shall number the Provinces of his Dominion with
the Arabic Numerals, 1, 2, 3, &c., *ad finem*. And he
shall instruct and direct his Grand Exchequer as to
the appropriation and disbursement of the revenue
of the * that comes to his hands. He shall have
power to appoint his Furies; also to appoint a Grand
Scribe and a Grand Exchequer for his department,
and appoint and ordain Special Deputy Grand Titans to assist him in the more rapid and effectual
dissemination and establishment of the * throughout his Dominion. He shall have further power to
appoint and instruct Deputies to organize and control Provinces and Dens, until the same shall elect
a Grand Giant and a Grand Cyclops, in the manner hereinafter provided.

GRAND GIANT.

Sec. 4. It shall be the duty of the Grand Giant,
who is the Chief Officer of the Province, to supervise and administer general and special instruction in the formation and establishment of
*s within his Province, and to report to the Grand
Titan, when required by that officer, the condition,
strength, progress and efficiency of the * throughout his Province, and to transmit, through the
Grand Cyclops, to the subordinate *s of his Province, all information or intelligence conveyed to
him by the Grand Titan for that purpose, and such
other information and instruction as he may think

Fide non armis.

will advance the interests of the *. He shall keep by
his G. Scribe a list of the names (without caption) of
the Grand Cyclops of the various Dens of his Province, and shall report the same to the Grand Titan
when required; and shall number the Dens of his
Province with the Arabic numerals, 1, 2, 3, &c., *ad
finem.* And shall determine and limit the number
of Dens to be organized in his Province. And he
shall instruct and direct his Grand Exchequer as to
what appropriation and disbursement he shall make
of the revenue of the * that comes to his hands.
He shall have power to appoint his Goblins; also,
a Grand Scribe and a Grand Exchequer for his department, and to appoint and ordain Special Deputy Grand Giants to assist him in the more rapid
and effectual dissemination and establishment of
the * throughout his Province. He shall have
the further power to appoint and instruct Deputies
to organize and control Dens, until the same shall
elect a Grand Cyclops in the manner hereinafter
provided. And in all cases, he shall preside at and
conduct the Grand Council of Yahoos.

GRAND CYCLOPS.

Sec. 5. It shall be the duty of the Grand Cyclops
to take charge of the * of his Den after his election,
under the direction and with the assistance (when
practicable) of the Grand Giant, and in accordance
with, and in conformity to the provisions of this
Prescript, a copy of which shall in all cases be obtained before the formation of a * begins. It shall further be his duty to appoint all regular meetings of
his * and to preside at the same—to appoint irregular meetings when he deems it expedient, to preserve
order in his Den, and to impose fines for irregularities
or disobedience of orders, and to receive and initiate
candidates for admission into the * after the
same shall have been pronounced competent and wor-

Hic manent vestigia morientis libertatis.

thy to become members by the Investigating Committee. He shall make a quarterly report to the
Grand Giant, of the condition, strength and efficiency of the * of his Den, and shall convey to
the Ghouls of his Den, all information or intelligence conveyed to him by the Grand Giant for that
purpose, and all other such information or instruction as he may think will conduce to the interests
and welfare of the *. He shall preside at and conduct the Grand Council of Centaurs. He shall have
power to appoint his Night Hawks, his Grand
Scribe, his Grand Turk, his Grand Sentinel, and
his Grand Ensign. And he shall instruct and direct the Grand Exchequer of his Den, as to what
appropriation and disbursement he shall make of
the revenue of the * that comes to his hands.
And for any small offense he may punish any member by fine, and may reprimand him for the same:
And he may admonish and reprimand the * of
his Den for any imprudence, irregularity or transgression, when he is convinced or advised that the
interests, welfare and safety of the * demand it.

GRAND MAGI.

Sec. 6. It shall be the duty of the Grand Magi,
who is the Second Officer, in Authority, of the Den,
to assist the Grand Cyclops and to obey all the
proper orders of that officer. To preside at all
meetings in the Den in the absence of the Grand
Cyclops; and to exercise during his absence all the
powers and authority conferred upon that officer.

GRAND MONK.

Sec. 7. It shall be the duty of the Grand Monk,
who is the third officer, in authority, of the Den, to
assist and obey all the proper orders of the Grand
Cyclops and the Grand Magi. And in the absence
of both of these officers, he shall preside at and conduct the meetings in the Den, and shall exercise all

8]   Cessante causa, cessat effectus.

the powers and authority conferred upon the Grand
Cyclops.

GRAND EXCHEQUER.

Sec. 8. It shall be the duty of the Grand Exchequers of the different Departments of the * to keep
a correct account of all the revenue of the * that
shall come to their hands, and shall make no appropriation or disbursement of the same except under
the orders and direction of the chief officer of their
respective departments. And it shall further be
the duty of the Grand Exchequer of Dens to collect
the initiation fees, and all fines imposed by the
Grand Cyclops.

GRAND TURK.

Sec. 9. It shall be the duty of the Grand Turk,
who is the Executive Officer of the Grand Cyclops,
to notify the ghouls of the Den of all informal or
irregular meetings appointed by the Grand Cyclops
and to obey and execute all the lawful orders of that
officer in the control and government of his Den.
It shall further be his duty to receive and question
at the Out Posts, all candidates for admission into
the *, and shall *there* administer the preliminary
obligation required, and then to conduct such candidate or candidates to the Grand Cyclops at his
Den, and to assist him in the initiation of the same.
And it shall further be his duty to act as the executive officer of the Grand Council of Centaurs.

GRAND SCRIBE.

Sec. 10. It shall be the duty of the Grand Scribes
of the different departments to conduct the correspondence and write the orders of the chiefs of their
departments, when required. And it shall further
be the duty of the Grand Scribes of the Den to keep
a list of the names (without caption) of the ghouls
of the Den—to call the Roll at all regular meetings
and to make the quarterly report under the direction of the Grand Cyclops.

Droit et avant.

Cave quid dicis, quando, et cui.   [9

GRAND SENTINEL.

Sec. 11. It shall be the duty of the Grand Sentinel to detail, take charge of, post and instruct the Grand Guard under the direction and orders of the Grand Cyclops, and to relieve and dismiss the same when directed by that officer.

GRAND ENSIGN.

Sec. 12. It shall be the duty of the Grand Ensign to take charge of the Grand Banner of the *, to preserve it sacredly, and protect it carefully, and to bear it on all occasions of parade or ceremony, and on such other occasions as the Grand Cyclops may direct it to be flung to the night breeze.

ELECTION OF OFFICERS.

ART. V. Sec. 1. The Grand Cyclops, the Grand Magi, the Grand Monk, and the Grand Exchequer of Dens, shall be elected semi-annually by the ghouls of Dens. And the first election for these officers may take place as soon as seven ghouls have been initiated for that purpose.

Sec. 2. The Grand Wizard of the Empire, the Grand Dragons of Realms, the Grand Titans of Dominions, and the Grand Giants of Provinces, shall be elected biennially, and in the following manner, to wit: The Grand Wizard by a majority vote of the Grand Dragons of his Empire, the Grand Dragons by a like vote of the Grand Titans of his Realm; the Grand Titans by a like vote of the Grand Giants of his Dominion, and the Grand Giant by a like vote of the Grand Cyclops of his Province.

The first election for Grand Dragon may take place as soon as three Dominions have been organized in a Realm, but all subsequent elections shall be by a majority vote of the Grand Titans, throughout the Realm. and biennially as aforesaid.

The first election for Grand Titan may take place

Dormitur aliquando jus, moritur nunquam.

as soon as three Provinces have been organized in a
Dominion, but all subsequent elections shall be by a
majority vote of all the Grand Giants throughout
the Dominion and biennially as aforesaid.

The first election for Grand Giant may take place
as soon as three Dens have been organized in a
Province, but all subsequent elections shall be by a
majority vote of all the Grand Cyclops throughout
the Province, and biennially as aforesaid.

The Grand Wizard of the Empire is hereby created, to serve three years from the First Monday
in May, 1867, after the expiration of which time,
biennial elections shall be held for that office as
aforesaid. And the incumbent Grand Wizard shall
notify the Grand Dragons, at least six months before said election, at what time and place the same
will be held.

JUDICIARY.

ART. VI. Sec. 1. The Tribunal of Justice of this
* shall consist of a Grand Council of Yahoos, and
a Grand Council of Centaurs.

Sec. 2. The Grand Council of Yahoos, shall be
the Tribunal for the trial of all elected officers, and
shall be composed of officers of equal rank with the
accused, and shall be appointed and presided over
by an officer of the next rank above, and sworn by
him to administer even handed justice. The Tribunal for the trial of the Grand Wizard, shall be composed of all the Grand Dragons of the Empire, and
shall be presided over and sworn by the senior
Grand Dragon. They shall have power to summon
the accused, and witnesses for and against him, and
if found guilty they shall prescribe the penalty and
execute the same. And they shall have power to
appoint an executive officer to attend said Council
while in session.

Sec. 3. The Grand Council of Centaurs shall be the Tribunal for the trial of Ghouls and non-elective officers, and shall be composed of six judges appointed by the Grand Cyclops from the Ghouls of his Den, presided over and sworn by him to give the accused a fair and impartial trial. They shall have power to summon the accused, and witnesses for and against him, and if found guilty they shall prescribe the penalty and execute the same. Said Judges shall be selected by the Grand Cyclops with reference to their intelligence, integrity and fair-mindedness, and shall render their verdict without prejudice or partiality.

REVENUE.

ART. VII. Sec. 1. The revenue of this * shall be derived as follows: For every copy of this Prescript issued to the *s of Dens, Ten Dollars will be required. Two dollars of which shall go into the hands of the Grand Exchequer of the Grand Giant; two into the hands of the Grand Exchequer of the Grand Titan; two into the hands of the Grand Exchequer of the Grand Dragon, and the remaining four into the hands of the Grand Exchequer of the Grand Wizard.

Sec. 2. A further source of revenue to the Empire shall be ten per cent. of all the revenue of the Realms, and a tax upon Realms, when the Grand Wizard shall deem it necessary and indispensable to levy the same.

Sec. 3. A further source of revenue to Realms shall be ten per cent. of all the revenue of Dominions, and a tax upon Dominions when the Grand Dragon shall deem such tax necessary and indispensable.

Sec. 4. A further source of revenue to Dominions shall be ten per cent. of all the revenue of Provinces, and a tax upon Provinces when the Grand Titan shall deem such tax necessary and indispensable.

Sec. 5. A further source of revenue to Provinces shall be ten per cent. on all the revenue of Dens, and a tax upon the Dens, when the Grand Giant shall deem such tax necessary and indispensable.

Sec. 6. The source of revenue to Dens, shall be the initiation fees, fines, and a *per capita* tax, whenever the Grand Cyclops shall deem such tax indispensable to the interests and purposes of the *.

Sec. 7. All of the revenue obtained in the manner herein aforesaid, shall be for the exclusive benefit of the *. And shall be appropriated to the dissemination of the same, and to the creation of a fund to meet any disbursement that it may become necessary to make to accomplish the objects of the *, and to secure the protection of the same.

OBLIGATION.

ART. VIII. No one shall become a member of this *, unless he shall take the following oath or obligation:

"I, ———— of my own free will and accord, and in the presence of Almighty God, do solemnly swear or affirm that I will never reveal to any one, not a member of the * * by any intimation, sign, symbol, word or act, or in any other manner whatever, any of the secrets, signs, grips, pass words, mysteries or purposes of the * * or that I am a member of the same or that I know any one who *is* a member, and that I will abide by the Prescript and Edicts of the * *. So help me God."

Sec. 2. The preliminary obligation to be administered before the candidate for admission is taken to the Grand Cyclops for examination, shall be as follows:

"I do solemnly swear or affirm that I will never

Tempora mutantur, et nos mutamur in illis.   [13

reveal any thing that I may this day (or night) learn concerning the * *. So help me God."

ADMISSION.

ART. IX. Sec. 1. No one shall be presented for admission into this *, until he shall have been recommended by some friend or intimate, who *is* a member, to the Investigating Committee, which shall be composed of the Grand Cyclops, the Grand Magi and the Grand Monk, and who shall investigate his antecedents and his past and present standing and connections, and if after such investigation, they pronounce him competent and worthy to become a member, he may be admitted upon taking the obligation required and passing through the ceremonies of initiation. *Provided,* That no one shall be admitted into this * who shall have not attained the age of eighteen years.

Sec. 2. No one shall become a member of a distant * when there is a * established and in operation in his own immediate vicinity. Nor shall any one become a member of any * after he shall have been rejected by any other *.

ENSIGN.

ART. X. The Grand Banner of this * shall be in the form of an isosceles triangle, five feet long and three wide at the staff. The material shall be Yellow, with a Red scalloped border, about three inches in width. There shall be painted upon it, in black, a Dracovolans, or Flying Dragon,† with the following motto inscribed above the Dragon, "QUOD SEMPER, QUOD UBIQUE, QUOD AB OMNIBUS."‡

AMENDMENTS.

ART. XI. This Prescript or any part or Edicts thereof, shall never be changed except by a two-

---

†See Webster's Unabridged Pictorial.
‡"What always, what every where, what by all is held to be true."

O tempora! O mores!

thirds vote of the Grand Dragons of the Realms, in Convention assembled, and at which Convention the Grand Wizard shall preside and be entitled to a vote. And upon the application of a majority of the Grand Dragons, for that purpose, the Grand Wizard shall appoint the time and place for said Convention; which, when assembled, shall proceed to make such modifications and amendments as it may think will advance the interest, enlarge the utility and more thoroughly effectuate the purposes of the *.

INTERDICTION.

ART. XII. The origin, designs, mysteries and ritual of this * shall never be written, but the same shall be communicated orally.

REGISTER.

1st—Dismal.	7th—Dreadful.
2nd—Dark.	8th—Terrible.
3rd—Furious.	9th—Horrible.
4th—Portentous.	10th—Melancholy.
5th—Wonderful.	11th—Mournful.
6th—Alarming.	12th—Dying.

II.

I—White.	IV—Black.
II—Green.	V—Yellow.
III—Blue.	VI—Crimson.

VII—Purple.

III.

1—Fearful.	7—Doleful.
2—Startling.	8—Sorrowful.
3—Awful.	9—Hideous.
4—Woeful.	10—Frightful.
5—Horrid.	11—Appalling.
6—Bloody.	12—Last.

EDICTS.

I. The Initiation Fee of this * shall be one dollar, to be paid when the candidate is initiated and received into the *.

II. No member shall be allowed to take any intoxicating spirits to any meeting of the *. Nor shall any member be allowed to attend a meeting when intoxicated; and for every appearance at a meeting in such a condition, he shall be fined the sum of not less than one nor more than five dollars, to go into the revenue of the *.

III. Any member may be expelled from the * by a majority vote of the officers and ghouls of the Den to which he belongs, and if after such expulsion such member shall assume any of the duties, regalia or insignia of the * or in any way claim to be a member of the same, he shall be severely punished. His obligation of secrecy shall be as binding upon him after expulsion as before, and for any revelation made by him thereafter, he shall be held accountable in the same manner as if he were then a member.

IV. Every Grand Cyclops shall read or cause to be read, this Prescript and these Edicts to the * of his Den, at least once in every three months,— And shall read them to each new member when he is initiated, or present the same to him for personal perusal.

V. Each Den may provide itself with the Grand Banner of the *.

VI. The *s of Dens may make such additional Edicts for their control and government as they shall deem requisite and necessary. *Provided,* No Edict shall be made to conflict with any of the provisions or Edicts of this Prescript.

VII. The strictest and most rigid secrecy, concerning any and everything that relates to the * shall at all times be maintained.

VIII. Any member who shall reveal or betray the secrets or purposes of this * shall suffer the extreme penalty of the Law.

Hush, thou art not to utter what
I am. Bethink thee; it was our covenant.
I said that I would see thee once again.

Ne quid detrimenti Respublica capiat.

16]   Amici usque ad aras.

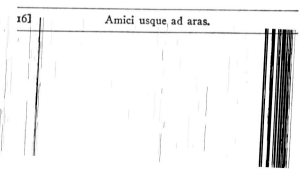

L' ENVOI.

To the lovers of Law and Order, Peace and Justice, we send greeting; and to the shades of the venerated Dead, we affectionately dedicate the * *

Nos ducit amor libertatis.

APPENDIX II.

REVISED AND AMENDED PRE-SCRIPT OF KU KLUX KLAN

ADOPTED IN 1868 (?)

Reprinted *in facsimile*

REVISED AND AMENDED

PRESCRIPT

OF THE

ORDER

OF THE

* * *

Damnant quod non intelligunt.

APPELLATION.

THIS Organization shall be styled and denominated, the Order of the * * *

CREED.

WE, the Order of the * * *, reverentially acknowledge the majesty and supremacy of the Divine Being, and recognize the goodness and providence of the same. And we recognize our relation to the United States Government, the supremacy of the Constitution, the Constitutional Laws thereof, and the Union of States thereunder.

CHARACTER AND OBJECTS OF THE ORDER.

THIS is an institution of Chivalry, Humanity, Mercy, and Patriotism; embodying in its genius and its principles all that is chivalric in conduct, noble in sentiment, generous in manhood, and patriotic in purpose; its peculiar objects being

First: To protect the weak, the innocent, and the defenceless, from the indignities, wrongs, and outrages of the lawless, the violent, and the brutal; to relieve the injured and oppressed; to succor the suffering and unfortunate, and especially the widows and orphans of Confederate soldiers.

Second: To protect and defend the Constitution of the United States, and all laws passed in conformity thereto, and to protect the States and the people thereof from all invasion from any source whatever.

Third: To aid and assist in the execution of all constitutional laws, and to protect the people from unlawful seizure, and from trial except by their peers in conformity to the laws of the land,

ARTICLE I.

TITLES.

SECTION 1. The officers of this Order shall consist of a Grand Wizard of the Empire, and his ten Genii; a Grand Dragon of the Realm,

3

and his eight Hydras; a Grand Titan of the Do-
minion, and his six Furies; a Grand Giant of
the Province, and his four Goblins; a Grand
Cyclops of the Den, and his two Night-hawks; a
Grand Magi, a Grand Monk, a Grand Scribe, a
Grand Exchequer, a Grand Turk, and a Grand
Sentinel.

SEC. 2. The body politic of this Order shall
be known and designated as "Ghouls."

ARTICLE II.

TERRITORY AND ITS DIVISIONS.

SECTION 1. The territory embraced within the
jurisdiction of this Order shall be coterminous
with the States of Maryland, Virginia, North
Carolina, South Carolina, Georgia, Florida, Alabama, Mississippi, Louisiana, Texas, Arkansas,
Missouri, Kentucky, and Tennessee; all combined constituting the Empire.

SEC. 2. The Empire shall be divided into four
departments, the first to be styled the Realm,
and coterminus with the boundaries of the
several States; the second to be styled the Dominion, and to be coterminous with such counties as the Grand Dragons of the several Realms
may assign to the charge of the Grand Titan.
The third to be styled the Province, and to be coterminous with the several counties; *provided,*
the Grand Titan may, when he deems it necessary, assign two Grand Giants to one Province,
prescribing, at the same time, the jurisdiction of

each. The fourth department to be styled the Den, and shall embrace such part of a Province as the Grand Giant shall assign to the charge of a Grand Cyclops.

ARTICLE III.
POWERS AND DUTIES OF OFFICERS.
GRAND WIZARD.

SECTION 1. The Grand Wizard, who is the supreme officer of the Empire, shall have power, and he shall be required to, appoint Grand Dragons for the different Realms of the Empire; and he shall have power to appoint his Genii, also a Grand Scribe, and a Grand Exchequer for his Department. and he shall have the sole power to issue copies of this Prescript, through his subalterns, for the organization and dissemination of the Order; and when a question of paramount importance to the interests or prosperity of the Order arises, not provided for in this Prescript, he shall have power to determine such question, and his decision shall be final until the same shall be provided for by amendment as hereinafter provided. It shall be his duty to communicate with, and receive reports from, the Grand Dragons of Realms, as to the condition, strength, efficiency, and progress of the Order within their respective Realms. And it shall further be his duty to keep, by his Grand Scribe, a list of the names (without any caption or explanation whatever) of the Grand Dragons of the different Realms of the Empire, and shall

6 *Quæmcunque miserum videris, hominem scias.*

number such Realms with the Arabic numerals
1, 2, 3, etc., *ad finem*; and he shall direct and
instruct his Grand Exchequer as to the appropriation and disbursement he shall make of the
revenue of the Order that comes to his hands.

GRAND DRAGON.

SEC. 2. The Grand Dragon, who is the chief
officer of the Realm, shall have power, and he
shall be required, to appoint and instruct a Grand
Titan for each Dominion of his Realm, (such
Dominion not to exceed three in number for any
Congressional District) said appointments being
subject to the approval of the Grand Wizard of
the Empire. He shall have power to appoint
his Hydras; also, a Grand Scribe and a Grand
Exchequer for his Department.

It shall be his duty to report to the Grand
Wizard, when required by that officer, the condition, strength, efficiency, and progress of the
Order within his Realm, and to transmit,
through the Grand Titan, or other authorized
sources, to the Order, all information, intelligence, or instruction conveyed to him by the
Grand Wizard for that purpose, and all such
other information or instruction as he may think
will promote the interest and utility of the Order. He shall keep by his Grand Scribe, a list
of the names (without caption) of the Grand
Titans of the different Dominions of his Realm,
and shall report the same to the Grand Wizard
when required, and shall number the Domin-

ion of his Realm with the Arabic numerals 1, 2, 3, etc., *ad finem.* And he shall direct and instruct his Grand Exchequer as to the appropriation and disbursement he shall make of the revenue of the Order that comes to his hands.

GRAND TITAN.

SEC. 3. The Grand Titan, who is the chief officer of the Dominion, shall have power, and he shall be required, to appoint and instruct a Grand Giant for each Province of his Dominion, such appointments, however, being subject to the approval of the Grand Dragon of the Realm. He shall have the power to appoint his Furies; also, a Grand Scribe and a Grand Exchequer for his Department. It shall be his duty to report to the Grand Dragon when required by that officer, the condition, strength, efficiency, and progress of the Order within his Dominion, and to transmit through the Grand Giant, or other authorized channels, to the Order, all information, intelligence, instruction or directions conveyed to him by the Grand Dragon for that purpose, and all such other information or instruction as he may think will enhance the interest or efficiency of the Order.

He shall keep, by his Grand Scribe, a list of the names (without caption or explanation) of the Grand Giants of the different Provinces of his Dominion, and shall report the same to the Grand Dragon when required; and shall number the Provinces of his Dominion with the Arabic numerals I, 2, 3, etc., *ad finem.* And he shall direct and instruct his Grand Exchequer as to the appropriation and disbursement he shall make of the revenue of the Order that comes to his hands.

GRAND GIANT.

SEC. 4. The Grand Giant, who is the chief officer of the Province, shall have power, and he is required, to appoint and instruct a Grand Cyclops for each Den of his Province, such appointments, however, being subject to the approval of the Grand Titan of the Dominion. And he shall have the further power to appoint his Goblins; also, a Grand Scribe and a Grand Exchequer for his Department.

It shall be his duty to supervise and administer general and special instructions in the organization and establishment of the Order within his Province, and to report to the Grand Titan, when required by that officer, the condition, strength, efficiency, and progress of the Order within his Province, and to transmit through the Grand Cyclops, or other legitimate sources, to the Order, all information, intelligence, instruction, or directions conveyed to him by the Grand Titan or other higher authority for that purpose, and all such other information or instruction as he may think would advance the purposes or prosperity of the Order. He shall keep, by his Grand Scribe, a list of the names (without cap-

tion or explanation) of the Grand Cyclops of the
various Dens of his Province, and shall report
the same to the Grand Titan when required; and
shall number the Dens of his Province with the
Arabic numerals 1, 2, 3, etc., *ad finem.* He
shall determine and limit the number of Dens
to be organized and established in his Province;
and he shall direct and instruct his Grand Exchequer as to the appropriation and disbursement he shall make of the revenue of the Order
that comes to his hands.

GRAND CYCLOPS.

Sec. 5. The Grand Cyclops, who is the chief
officer of the Den, shall have power to appoint
his Night-hawks, his Grand Scribe, his Grand
Turk, his Grand Exchequer, and his Grand Sentinel. And for small offenses he may punish
any member by fine, and may reprimand him
for the same. And he is further empowered to
admonish and reprimand his Den, or any of the
members thereof, for any imprudence, irregularity, or transgression, whenever he may think
that the interests, welfare, reputation or safety
of the Order demand it. It shall be his duty to
take charge of his Den under the instruction and
with the assistance (when practicable) of the
Grand Giant, and in accordance with and in conformity to the provisions of this Prescript—a
copy of which shall in all cases be obtained before the formation of a Den begins. It shall

further be his duty to appoint all regular meetings of his Den, and to preside at the same; to appoint irregular meetings when he deems it expedient; to preserve order and enforce discipline in his Den; to impose fines for irregularities or disobedience of orders; and to receive and initiate candidates for admission into the Order, after the same shall have been pronounced competent and worthy to become members, by the Investigating Committee herein after provided for. And it shall further be his duty to make a quarterly report to the Grand Giant of the condition, strength, efficiency, and progress of his Den, and shall communicate to the Officers and Ghouls of his Den, all information, intelligence, instruction, or direction, conveyed to him by the Grand Giant or other higher authority for that purpose; and shall from time to time administer all such other counsel, instruction or direction, as in his sound discretion, will conduce to the interests, and more effectually accomplish, the *real* objects and designs of the Order.

GRAND MAGI.

SEC. 6. It shall be the duty of the Grand Magi, who is the second officer in authority of the Den, to assist the Grand Cyclops, and to obey all the orders of that officer; to preside at all meetings in the Den, in the absence of the Grand Cyclops; and to discharge during his absence all the duties and exercise all the powers and authority of that officer.

Dormitus aliquando jus, moritus nunquam. **11**

GRAND MONK.

SEC. 7. It shall be the duty of the Grand Monk, who is the third officer in authority of the Den, to assist and obey all the orders of the Grand Cyclops and the Grand Magi; and, in the absence of both of these officers, he shall preside at and conduct the meetings in the Den, and shall discharge all the duties, and exercise all the powers and authority of the Grand Cyclops.

GRAND EXCHEQUER.

SEC. 8. It shall be the duty of the Grand Exchequers of the different Departments to keep a correct account of all the revenue of the Order that comes to their hands, and of all paid out by them; and shall make no appropriation or disbursement of the same except under the orders and direction of the chief officer of their respective Departments. And it shall further be the duty of the Exchequers of Dens to collect the initiation fees, and all fines imposed by the Grand Cyclops, or the officer discharging his functions.

GRAND TURK.

SEC. 9 It shall be the duty of the Grand Turk, who is the executive officer of the Grand Cyclops, to notify the Officers and Ghouls of the Den, of all informal or irregular meetings appointed by the Grand Cyclops, and to obey and execute all the orders of that officer in the control and government of his Den. It shall further be his duty to receive and question at the outposts, all candidates for admission into the Order, and shall *there* administer the preliminary obligation required, and then to conduct such candidate or candidates to the Grand Cyclops, and to assist him in the initiation of the same.

GRAND SCRIBE.

SEC. 10. It shall be the duty of the Grand Scribes of the different Departments to conduct the correspondence and write the orders of the Chiefs of their Departments, when required. And it shall further be the duty of the Grand Scribes of Dens, to keep a list of the names (without any caption or explanation whatever) of the Officers and Ghouls of the Den, to call the roll at all meetings, and to make the quarterly reports under the direction and instruction of the Grand Cyclops.

GRAND SENTINEL

SEC. 11. It shall be the duty of the Grand Sentinel to take charge of post, and instruct the Grand Guard, under the direction and orders of the Grand Cyclops, and to relieve and dismiss the same when directed by that officer.

THE STAFF.

SEC. 12. The Genii shall constitute the staff of the Grand Wizard; the Hydras, that of the Grand Dragon; the Furies, that of the Grand Titan; the Goblins, that of the Grand Giant; and the Night-hawks, that of the Grand Cyclops.

REMOVAL.

SEC. 13. For any just, reasonable and substantial cause, any appointee may be removed by the authority that appointed him, and his place supplied by another appointment.

ARTICLE IV
ELECTION OF OFFICERS.

SECTION 1. The Grand Wizard shall be elected biennially by the Grand Dragons of Realms. The first election for this office to take place on the 1st Monday in May, 1870, (a Grand Wizard having been created, by the original Prescript, to serve three years from the 1st Monday in May, 1867); all subsequent elections to take place every two years thereafter. And the incumbent Grand Wizard shall notify the Grand Dragons of the different Realms, at least six months before said election, at what time and place the same will be held; a majority vote of all the Grand Dragons *present* being necessary and sufficient to elect a Grand Wizard. Such election shall be by ballot, and shall be held by three Commissioners appointed by the Grand Wizard for that purpose; and in the event of a tie, the Grand Wizard shall have the casting-vote.

SEC. 2. The Grand Magi and the Grand Monk of Dens shall be elected annually by the Ghouls of Dens; and the first election for these officers may take place as soon as ten Ghouls have been initiated for the formation of a Den. All subse-

14.   *Art est colare artem.*

quent elections to take place every year thereafter.

Sec. 3. In the event of a vacancy in the office
of Grand Wizard, by death, resignation, removal,
or otherwise, the senior Grand Dragon of the
Empire shall immediately assume and enter
upon the discharge of the duties of the Grand
Wizard, and shall exercise the powers and perform the duties of said office until the same shall
be filled by election; and the said senior Grand
Dragon, as soon as practicable after the happen-
ing of such vacancy, shall call a convention o
the Grand Dragons of Realms, to be held at
such time and place as in his discretion he may
deem most convenient and proper. *Provided,*
however, that the time for assembling such Convention for the election of a Grand Wizard shall
in no case exceed six months from the time such
vacancy occurred; and in the event of a vacancy in any other office, the same shall immediately be filled in the manner herein before
mentioned.

Sec. 4. The Officers heretofore elected or appointed may retain their offices during the time
for which they have been so elected or appointed,
at the expiration of which time said offices shall
be filled as herein-before provided.

ARTICLE V
JUDICIARY.

Section 1. The Tribunal of Justice of this
Order shall consist of a Court at the Head-quar-

ters of the Empire, the Realm, the Dominion, the Province, and the Den, to be appointed by the Chiefs of these several Departments.

SEC. 2. The Court at the Head-quarters of the Empire shall consist of three Judges for the trial of Grand Dragons, and the Officers and attachés belonging to the Head-quarters of the Empire.

SEC. 3. The Court at the Head-quarters of the Realm shall consist of three Judges for the trial, of Grand Titans, and the Officers and attachés belonging to the Head-quarters of the Realm.

SEC. 4. The Court at the Head-quarters of the Dominion shall consist of three Judges for the trial of Grand Giants, and the Officers and attachés belonging to the Head-quarters of the Dominion.

SEC. 5. The Court at the Head-quarters of the Province shall consist of five Judges for the trial of Grand Cyclops, the Grand Magis, Grand Monks, and the Grand Exchequers of Dens, and the Officers and attachés belonging to the Head-quarters of the Province.

SEC. 6. The Court at the Head-quarters of the Den shall consist of seven Judges appointed from the Den for the trial of Ghouls and the officers belonging to the Head quarters of the Den.

SEC. 7. The Tribunal for the trial of the Grand Wizard shall be composed of at least seven Grand Dragons, to be convened by the senior Grand Dragon upon charges being preferred against the

Grand Wizard; which Tribunal shall be organized and presided over by the senior Grand Dragon *present;* and if they find the accused guilty, they shall prescribe the penalty, and the senior Grand Dragon of the Empire shall cause the same to be executed.

SEC. 8. The aforesaid Courts shall summon the accused and witnesses for and against him, and if found guilty, they shall prescribe the penalty, and the Officers convening the Court shall cause the same to be executed. *Provided* the accused shall always have the right of appeal to the next Court above, whose decision shall be final.

SEC. 9. The Judges constituting the aforesaid Courts shall be selected with reference to their intelligence, integrity, and fair-mindedness, and shall render their verdict without prejudice, favor, partiality, or affection, and shall be so sworn, upon the organization of the Court; and shall further be sworn to administer even-handed justice.

SEC. 10. The several Courts herein provided for shall be governed in their deliberations, proceedings, and judgments by the rules and regulations governing the proceedings of regular Courts-martial.

ARTICLE VI.
REVENUE.

SECTION 1. The revenue of this Order shall be derived as follows: For every copy of this Prescript issued to Dens, $10 will be required; $2 of which shall go into the hands of the Grand Exchequer of the Grand Giant, $2 into the hands of the Grand Exchequer of the Grand Titan, $2 into the hands of the Grand Exchequer of the Grand Dragon, and the remaining $4 into the hands of the Grand Exchequer of the Grand Wizard.

SEC. 2. A further source of revenue to the Empire shall be ten per cent. of all the revenue of the Realms, and a tax upon Realms when the Grand Wizard shall deem it necessary and indispensable to levy the same.

SEC. 3. A further source of revenue to Realms shall be ten per cent. of all the revenue of Dominions, and a tax upon Dominions when the Grand Dragon shall deem it necessary and indispensable to levy the same.

SEC. 4. A further source of revenue to Dominions shall be ten per cent. of all the revenue of Provinces, and a tax upon Provinces when the Grand Giant shall deem such tax necessary and indispensable.

SEC. 5. A further source of revenue to Provinces shall be ten per cent. of all the revenue of Dens, and a tax upon Dens when the Grand Giant shall deem such tax necessary and indispensable.

SEC. 6. The source of revenue to Dens shall be the initiation fees, fines, and a *per capita* tax, whenever the Grand Cyclops shall deem such tax necessary and indispensable to the interests and objects of the Order.

SEC. 7. All the revenue obtained in the manner aforesaid, shall be for the *exclusive* benefit of the Order, and shall be appropriated to the dissemination of the same and to the creation of a fund to meet any disbursement that it may become necessary to make to accomplish the objects of the Order and to secure the protection of the same.

ARTICLE VII.

ELIGIBILITY FOR MEMBERSHIP.

SECTION 1. No one shall be presented for admission into the Order until he shall have first been recommended by some friend or intimate who *is* a member, to the Investigating Committee, (which shall be composed of the Grand Cyclops, the Grand Magi, and the Grand Monk,) and who shall have investigated his antecedents and his past and present standing and connections; and after such investigation, shall have pronounced him competent and worthy to become a member.   *Provided*, no one shall be presented for admission into, or become a member of, this Order who shall not have attained the age of eighteen years.

SEC. 2. No one shall become a member of this Order unless he shall *voluntarily* take the following oaths or obligations, and shall *satisfactorily* answer the following interrogatories, while kneel-

ing, with his right hand raised to heaven, and
his left hand resting on the Bible:

PRELIMINARY OBLIGATION.

" I ——— solemnly swear or affirm that I will
never reveal any thing that I may this day (or
night) learn concerning the Order of the * * *,
and that I will true answer make to such interrogatories as may be put to me touching my com-
petency for admission into the same. So help
me God. "

INTERROGATORIES TO BE ASKED:

1st. Have you ever been rejected, upon application for membership in the * * *, or have you
ever been expelled from the same?

2d. Are you now, or have you ever been, a
member of the Radical Republican party, or
either of the organizations known as the "Loyal
League" and the "Grand Army of the Republic?".

3d. Are you opposed to the principles and
policy of the Radical party, and to the Loyal
League, and the Grand Army of the Republic,
so far as you are informed of the character and
purposes of those organizations?

4th. Did you belong to the Federal army
during the late war, and fight against the South
during the existence of the same?

5th. Are you opposed to negro equality, both
social and political?

6th. Are you in favor of a white man's government in this country?

20 | *Nemo tenetur seipsum accusare.*

7th. Are you in favor of Constitutional liberty, and a Government of equitable laws instead of a Government of violence and oppression?

8th. Are you in favor of maintaining the Constitutional rights of the South?

9th. Are you in favor of the re-enfranchisement and emancipation of the white men of the South, and the restitution of the Southern people to all their rights, alike proprietary, civil, and political?

10th. Do you believe in the inalienable right of self-preservation of the people against the exercise of arbitrary and unlicensed power?

If the foregoing interrogatories are satisfactorily answered, and the candidate desires to go further (after something of the character and nature of the Order has thus been indicated to him) and to be admitted to the benefits, mysteries, secrets and purposes of the Order, he shall then be required to take the following final oath or obligation. But if said interrogatories are not satisfactorily answered, or the candidate declines to proceed further, he shall be discharged, after being solemnly admonished by the initiating officer of the deep secresy to which the oath already taken has bound him, and that the extreme penalty of the law will follow a violation of the same.

FINAL OBLIGATION.

"I ——— of my own free will and accord, and in the presence of Almighty God, do solemnly swear or affirm, that I will never reveal to any one not a member of the Order of the * * *, by any intimation, sign, symbol, word or act, or in any other manner whatever, any of the secrets, signs, grips, pass-words, or mysteries of the Order of the * * *, or that I am a member of the same, or that I know any one who *is* a member; and that I will abide by the Prescript and Edicts of the Order of the * * *. So help me God."

The initiating officer will then proceed to explain to the new members the character and objects of the Order, and introduce him to the mysteries and secrets of the same; and shall read to him this Prescript and the Edicts thereof, or present the same to him for personal perusal.

ARTICLE VIII.
AMENDMENTS.

This Prescript or any part or Edicts thereof shall never be changed, except by a two-thirds vote of the Grand Dragons of the Realms, in convention assembled, and at which convention the Grand Wizard shall preside and be entitled to a vote. And upon the application of a majority of the Grand Dragons for that purpose, the Grand Wizard shall call and appoint the time and place for said convention; which, when assembled, shall proceed to make such modifications and amendments as it may think will promote the interest, enlarge the utility, and more thoroughly effectuate the purposes of the Order

ARTICLE IX.

INTERDICTION.

The origin, mysteries, and Ritual of this Order shall never be written, but the same shall be communicated orally.

ARTICLE X.

EDICTS.

1. No one shall become a member of a distant Den, when there is a Den established and in operation in his own immediate vicinity; nor shall any one become a member of any Den, or of this Order in any way, after he shall have been once rejected, upon application for membership.

2. No Den, or officer, or member, or members thereof, shall operate beyond their prescribed limits, unless invited or ordered by the proper authority so to do.

3. No member shall be allowed to take any intoxicating spirits to any meeting of the Den; nor shall any member be allowed to attend a meeting while intoxicated; and for every appearance at a meeting in such condition, he shall be fined the sum of not less than one nor more than five dollars, to go into the revenue of the Order.

4. Any member may be expelled from the Order by a majority vote of the Officers and Ghouls of the Den to which he belongs; and if after such expulsion, such member shall assume any of the duties, regalia, or insignia of the Or-

der, or in any way claim to be a member of the
same, he shall be severely punished. His obligation of secrecy shall be as binding upon him
after expulsion as before, and for any revelation
made by him thereafter, he shall be held accountable in the same manner as if he were then
a member.

5. Upon the expulsion of any member from
the Order, the Grand Cyclops, or the officer acting in his stead, shall immediately report the
same to the Grand Giant of the Province, who
shall cause the fact to be made known and read
in each Den of his Province, and shall transmit
the same, through the proper channels, to the
Grand Dragon of the Realm, who shall cause it
to be published to every Den in his Realm, and
shall notify the Grand Dragons of contiguous
Realms of the same.

6. Every Grand Cyclops shall read, or cause
to be read, this Prescript and these Edicts to his
Den, at least once in every month; and shall read
them to each new member when he is initiated,
or present the same to him for personal perusal.

7. The initiation fee of this Order shall be one
dollar, to be paid when the candidate is initiated
and received into the Order.

8. Dens may make such additional Edicts for
their control and government as they may deem
requisite and necessary. *Provided*, no Edict
shall be made to conflict with any of the provisions or Edicts of this Prescript.

24.   *Ad unum omnes.*

9. The most profound and rigid secrecy concerning any and everything that relates to the Order, shall at all times be maintained.

10. Any member who shall reveal or betray the secrets of this Order, shall suffer the extreme penalty of the law.

ADMONITION.

Hush! thou art not to utter what I am; bethink thee! it was our covenant!

REGISTER.

I.

1. Dismal,	7. Painful,
2. Mystic,	8. Portentous,
3. Stormy,	9. Fading,
4. Peculiar,	10. Melancholy,
5. Blooming,	11. Glorious,
6. Brilliant,	12. Gloomy.

II.

I. White, II. Green, III. Yellow, IV. Amber, v. Purple, VI. Crimson, VII. Emerald.

III.

1. Fearful,	7. Hideous,
2. Startling,	8. Frightful,
3. Wonderful	9. Awful,
4. Alarming,	10. Horrible,
5. Mournful,	11. Dreadful,
6. Appalling,	12. Last.

IV.

Cumberland.

L'ENVOI.

To the lovers of law and order, peace and justice, we send greeting; and to the shades of the venerated dead we affectionately dedicate the Order of the * * *

Resurgamus.

APPENDIX III.

CONSTITUTION OF A LOCAL ORDER MODELED UPON KU KLUX KLAN

Used in South Carolina and in North Carolina

From The Ku Klux Report, North Carolina Testimony

CONSTITUTION

ARTICLE I.

This organization shall be known as the ———— Order, No. —, of the Ku Klux Klan of the State of South Carolina.

ARTICLE II.

The officers shall consist of a cyclops and a scribe, both of whom shall be elected by a majority vote of the order, and to hold their office during good behavior.

ARTICLE III.

Section 1. It shall be the duty of the C. to preside in the order, enforce a due observance of the constitution and by-laws, and an exact compliance to the rules and usages of the order; to see that all the members perform their respective duties; to appoint all committees before the order;

inspect the arms and dress of each member on special occasions; to call meetings when necessary; draw upon members for all sums needed to carry on the order.

Sec. 2.   The S. shall keep a record of the proceedings of the order; write communications; notify other Klans when their assistance is needed; give notice when any member has to suffer the penalty for violating his oath; see that all books, papers or other property belonging to his office, are placed beyond the reach of any one not a member of the order.   He shall perform such other duties as may be required of him by the C.

ARTICLE IV.

Section 1.   No person shall be initiated into this order under eighteen years of age.

Sec. 2.   No person of color shall be admitted into this order.

Sec. 3.   No person shall be admitted into this order who does not sustain a good moral character, and who is in any way incapacitated to perform the duties of a Ku Klux.

Sec. 4.   The name of a person proposed for membership must be proposed by the committee appointed by the chief, verbally, stating age, residence, and occupation; state if he was a soldier in the late war, his rank, whether in the Federal or Confederate service, and his command.

ARTICLE V.

SECTION 1. Any member who shall offend against these articles, or the by-laws shall be subject to be fined and reprimanded by the C., as two-thirds of the members present at any regular meeting may determine.

SEC. 2. Every member shall be entitled to a fair trial for any offense involving reprimand or criminal punishment.

BY-LAWS

ARTICLE I.

SECTION 1. This order shall meet at ————.

SEC. 2. Five members shall constitute a quorum, provided the C. or S. be present.

SEC. 3.   The C. shall have power to
appoint such members of the order to
attend the sick, the needy, and those dis-
tressed, and those suffering from radical
misrule, as the case may require.

SEC. 4.   No person shall be appointed
on a committee unless the person is present
at the time of appointment.   Members of
committees neglecting to report shall be
fined 30 cents.

ARTICLE II.

SECTION 1.   Every member, on being
admitted, shall sign the constitution and
by-laws and pay the initiation fee.

SEC. 2.   A brother of the Klan wishing
to become a member of this order, who
shall present his application with the
proper papers of transfer from the order
of which he was a member formerly, shall
be admitted to the order only by a unanimous vote of the members present.

ARTICLE III.

SECTION 1.   The initiation fee shall be
————————.

ARTICLE IV.

SECTION I.   Every member who shall refuse or neglect to pay his fine or dues shall be dealt with as the chief thinks proper.

SEC. 2.   Sickness or absence from the country or being engaged in any important business shall be a valid excuse for any neglect of duty.

ARTICLE V.

SECTION I.   Each member shall provide himself with a pistol, Ku Klux gown and signal instruments.

SEC. 2.   When charges have been preferred against a member in proper manner, or any matters of grievance between brother Ku Klux are brought before the order, they shall be referred to a committee of three or more members, who shall examine the parties and determine the matters in question, reporting their decision to the order.   If the parties interested desire, two-thirds of the members present voting in favor of the report, it shall be carried.

ARTICLE VI.

SECTION 1. It is the duty of every member who has evidence that another has violated Article II. to prefer the charges and specify the offense to the order.

SEC. 2. The charge for violating Article II. shall be referred to a committee of five or more members, who shall as soon as practicable, summon the parties and investigate the matter.

SEC. 3. If the committee agree that the charges are sustained, that the member on trial has intentionally violated his oath, or Article II., they shall report the fact to the order.

SEC. 4. If the committee agree that the charges are not sustained, that the member is not guilty of violating his oath or Article II., they shall report to that effect to the order and the charges shall be dismissed.

SEC. 5. When the committee report that the charges are sustained, and the unanimous vote of the members is given thereof, the offending person shall be sentenced to death by the chief.

SEC. 6. The person, through the cyclops of the order of which he is a member, can make application for pardon to the Great Grand Cyclops of Nashville, Tennessee, in which case execution of the sentence can be stayed until pardoning power is heard from.

ARTICLE VII.

SECTION 1. Any member who shall betray or divulge any of the matters of the order shall suffer death.

ARTICLE VIII.

SECTION 1. The following shall be the rules of any order to any matter herein not provided for; shall be managed in strict accordance with the Ku Klux rules.

SEC. 2. When the chief takes his position on the right, the scribe, with the members forming a half-circle around them, and at the sound of the signal instrument there shall be profound silence.

SEC. 3. Before proceeding to business, the scribe shall call the roll and note the absentees.

SEC. 4. Business shall be taken up in the following order:

1. Reading the minutes.

2. Excuse of members at preceding meeting.

3. Report of committee of candidates for membership.

4. Collection of dues.

5. Are any of the order sick or suffering?

6. Report of committees.

7. New business.

APPENDIX IV.

KU KLUX ORDERS, WARNINGS AND OATHS

KU KLUX ORDERS, WARN-
INGS, OATHS.

KU KLUX KLAN.

ALERT!

(Crossed muskets)
(and pistol.   )   (Spade ax ax.)

ALERT!   ALERT!

T   T   T   T   T   T   T   T   T   T

The B. G. C. of the K. K. K. is in town. You
who know the signal of his presence and have
seen it be on the *alert.* You who do not—to a
brother—*mark the nail of the finger and the*
(?)   must be organized in the future.
Traitors to their race *will not always flemish like
the bay. Dimity marks them. Look out. And
meet at the cave where the Greased Lightning
Slumbers.*

By order of the

B. G. C.

D. W. S.   In Pro., Per.

Forerunner.[1]

---

[1] Montgomery Mail, March 23, 1868.

KU KLUX.

Serpent's Den—Death's Retreat.
Hollow Tomb—Misery Cave of the
Great Ku Klux Kian, No. 1,000.
Windy Month—Bloody Moon,
Muddy Night—Twelfth Hour.

General Orders No. 1.

Make ready! Make ready! Make ready!
The mighty hobgoblins of the Confederate dead
in Hell-a-Bulloo assembled!
Revenge, Revenge!
Be secret, be cautious, be terrible!
By special grant, Hell freezes over for your
passage. Offended ghosts, put on your skates,
and cross over to mother earth!

Work! Work!! Work!!!
Double, double, toil and trouble;
Fire burn and cauldron bubble.

Ye white men who stick to black, soulless
beasts! the time arrives for you to part. Q. W.
X. W. V. U., and so, from Omega to Alpha.

Cool it with a baboon's blood
Then the charm is firm and good.

Ye niggers who stick to low whites!
Begone, Begone, Begone! The world turns
around—the thirteenth hour approacheth.
S. one, two, and three—beware! White and
yellow.
J. and T—— P—— and L—— begone.—The
handwriting on the wall warns you!

From the murderer's gibbet, throw
Into the flame. Come high and low.

By order of the Great
BLUFUSTIN.
A true copy,   G. S.   K. K. K.
Peterloo.
P. S.   K. K. K.

KU KLUX.

Hell-a-Bulloo Hole—Den of Skulls.
Bloody Bones—Headquarters of the
Great Ku Klux Klan, No. 1,000.
Windy Month—New Moon.
Cloudy Night--Thirteenth Hour.

General Orders No. 2.

The great chief Simulacre summons you!
Be ready! Crawl slowly! Strike hard!
Fire around the pot!
  Sweltered venom, sleeping got
  Boil thou first i' the charmed pot!
Like a hell-broth boil and bubble!
The Great High Priest Cyclops! C. J. F. Y.
Varnish, Tar and Turpentine!
The fifth Ghost sounds his Trumpet!
The mighty Genii wants two black wethers!
Make them, make them, make them! Presto!
The Great Giantess must have a white barrow.
Make him, make him, make him! Presto!
Meet at once—the den of Snakes—the Giants
jungle—the hole of Hell!
The second Hobgoblin will be there, a mighty
Ghost of valor! His eyes of fire, his voice of
thunder! Clean the streets—clean the serpents'
dens.
Red hot pincers! Bastinado!! Cut Clean!!!
No more to be born. Fire and brimstone.
Leave us, leave us, leave us! One, two, three
tonight! Others soon!
Hell freezes! On with skates — glide on.
Twenty from Atlanta. Call the roll. *Bene
dicite!* The Great Ogre orders it!
    By order of the Great
      BLUFUSTIN.
A true copy,   G. S. K. K. K.
  Peterloo.
P. S. K. K. K.

KU KLUX.

Hollow Hell, Devil's Den, Horrible
Shadows. Ghostly Sepulchre.
Head Quarters of the Immortal Ate
of the K. K. K. Gloomy month. Bloody
Moon. Black Night, Last Hour.

General Orders No. 3.

Shadowed Brotherhood! Murdered heroes!
Fling the bloody dirt that covers you to the four
winds! Erect thy Goddess on the banks of the
Avernus. Mark well your foes! Strike with the
red hot spear! Prepare Charon for his task!

Enemies reform! The skies shall be blackened!
A single Star shall look down upon horrible
deeds! The night owl shall hoot a requiem o'er
Ghostly Corpses!

Beware! Beware! Beware!

The Great Cyclops is angry! Hobgoblins report!
Shears and lash! Tar and Feathers! Hell and
Fury!

Revenge! Revenge! Revenge!

Bad men! white, black, yellow, repent!

The hour is at hand! Be ye ready! Life is
short. J. H. S. Y. W.!!!

Ghosts! Ghosts!! Ghosts!!!

Drink thy tea made of distilled hell, stirred with
the lightning of heaven, and sweetened with the
gall of thine enemies!

All will be well!!!

By order of the Great
BLUFUSTIN.

A true copy,   G. S.   K. K. K.

    Peterloo.

P. S.   K. K. K.[1]

---

[1] This and the two preceding orders were written by Ryland Randolph and printed in his paper
The Independent Monitor, of Tuscaloosa, Alabama.

THE FATE OF THE CARPETBAGGER AND THE SCALAWAG

Cartoon by Ryland Randolph in *Independent Monitor*, September 1, 1868.

TO THE PUBLIC.

K. K. K.

TAKEN BY HABEAS CORPUS.

In silence and secrecy thought has been working, and the benignant efficacies of concealment speak for themselves. Once again have we been forced by force to use *Force*. Justice was lame, and she had to lean upon us. Information being obtained that a "doubting Thomas," the inferior of nothing, the superior of nothing, and of consequence the equal of nothing, who has neither eyes to see the scars of oppression, nor ears to hear the cause of humanity, even though he wears the Judicial silk, had ordered some guilty prisoners from Union to the City of Columbia, and of injustice and prejudice, for an *unfair trial of life;* thus clutching at the wheel-spokes of destiny—then this thing was created and projected; otherwise it would never have been. We yield to the inevitable and inexorable, and account this the *best.* "Let not thy right hand know what thy left hand doeth," is our motto.

We want peace, but this cannot be till justice returns. We want and will have justice, but this cannot be till the bleeding fight of freedom is fought. Until then the Moloch of Iniquity will have his victims, even if the Michael of Justice must have his martyrs.

K. K. K.[1]

---

[1] From the *Weekly Union Times* of Unionville, S. C., February 17, 1871 ; South Carolina Testimony, pp. 1003, 1092. The negro militia of South Carolina had killed a man who refused to sell whisky to them. Several were arrested and imprisoned. A radical judge named Thomas, in Columbia, 60 or 70 miles away and out of the district where the crime was committed, directed that the prisoners be removed to Columbia for trial. The whites believed that this was done as the first step toward releasing the criminals. A mob came in, took the men from jail, shot them and gave to the sheriff the above notice with instructions to have it published in the newspapers.

ANOTHER KU KLUX PROCLAMATION.[1]

The following document was discovered on yesterday morning posted on the "legal advertisement" board hanging at the court-house door. We have examined the original and find it is in the same handwriting as the one left with the jailer on the night of the late raid on the jail:

HEADQUARTERS K. K. K., DEPARTMENT
OF S. C.,

General Orders No. 49

From the·G. G. C., S. S.

We delight not in speech, but there is language which, when meant in earnest, becomes desperate. We raise the voice of warning, beware! beware! Persons there are, (*and not unknown to us,*) who, to gratify some private grudge or selfish end, like Wheeler's men, so called, are executing their low, paltry, and pitiful designs at the expense, not only of the noble creed we profess and act, but also to the great trouble and annoyance of their neighbors in various communities. We stay our hand for once; but if such conduct is frightening away laborers, robbery, and connivance at the secrets of our organization is repeated, then the mockers *must* suffer and the traitors meet their merited doom. We dare not promise what we do not perform. We want no substitutes or conscripts in our ranks. We can be as generous as we are terrible; but, *stand back*. We've said it, and there can be no interference.

By order of the Grand Chief.

A. O.,
Grand Secretary.

_____

[1] *Weekly Union Times*, Unionville, S. C., February 24, 1871; Ku Klux Report, South Carolina Testimony, p. 1004. The Ku Klux Klan had many imitators, and lawless conduct was often carried on under the protection of the name and prestige of the Klan. The above warning was meant for those who had been using the name of the order to cloak evil deeds.

KU KLUX MANIFESTO.[1]

Below we publish a document which we received through the postoffice on Monday last, it having been dropped into the letter box the previous night, as we are informed by the postmaster. As to whether or not the paper is genuine, and emanates from the mysterious Ku Klux Klan, we have no means of knowing, as the handwriting is evidently disguised. Although it is our rule to decline the publication of all anonymous communications, we have decided to waive the rule in this instance, and print the document for what it is worth. Here it is in full:

EXTRACT OF MINUTES.

ARTICLE 1. Whereas there are malicious and evil disposed persons, who endeavor to perpetrate their malice, serve notices, and make threats under the cover of our august name, now we warn all such bogus organizations that we will not allow of any interference. Stop it.

ARTICLE 2. There shall be no interference with any honest, decent, well-behaved person, whether white or black; and we cordially invite all such to continue at their appropriate labor, and they shall be protected therein by the whole power of this organization. But we do intend that the honest, intelligent white people (the tax payers) of this county shall rule it! We can no longer put up with negro rule, black bayonets, and a miserably degraded, thievish set of lawmakers, (God save the mark!) the scum of the earth, the scrapings of creation. We are pledged to stop it; we are determined to end it, even if we are "forced by force to use force."

ARTICLE 3. Our attention having been called to the letter of one Rose, county treasurer of York,

---

[1] *Yorkville Enquirer,* Yorkville, S. C., March 9, 1871; South Carolina Testimony, p. 1347. Another warning to those engaged in lawlessness and using the name of the Klan.

we brand it as a lie! Our lieutenant was ordered to arrest him, that he might be tried on alleged charges of incendiarism, (and if convicted he will be executed). But there were no shots fired at him and no money stolen; that is not in our line, the legislature of the State of South Carolina have a monopoly in that line.

By command of the Chief.

Official: K. K. K., A. A. G.

K. K. K.[1]

HEADQUARTERS; NINTH DIVISION, S. C.,

Special Orders No. 3, *K. K. K.*

"Ignorance is the curse of God." For this reason we are determined that the members of the legislature, the school commissioners, and the county commissioners of Union, shall no longer officiate. Fifteen (15) days' notice from this date is therefore given and if they, *one and all,* do not *at once and forever resign* their present inhuman, disgraceful, and outrageous rule, then retributive justice will as surely be used as night follows day.

Also, "An honest man is the noblest work of God." For this reason, if the clerk of the said board of county commissioners and school commissioners does not *immediately* renounce and relinquish his present position, then harsher measures than these will most assuredly and *certainly* be used.

For confirmation, reference to the orders heretofore published in the *Union Weekly Times* and *Yorkville Enquirer* will more fully and completely show our intention.

A. O.,

March 9, 1871.   *Grand Secretary.*

---

[1] *Union Weekly Times,* March 17, 1871; South Carolina Testimony, p. 1096. This order illustrates one method of getting rid of obnoxious officials.

"Dam Your Soul. The Horrible *Sepulchre* and Bloody Moon has at last arrived. Some live to-day to-morrow "*Die.*" We the undersigned understand through our Grand "*Cyclops*" that you have recommended a big Black Nigger for Male agent on our role road; wel, sir, Jest you understand in time if he gets on the rode you can make up your mind to pull roape. If you have any thing to say in regard to the Matter, meet the Grand Cyclops and Conclave at Den No. 4 at 12 o'clock midnight, Oct. 1st, 1871.

"When you are in Calera we warn you to hold your tounge and not speak so much with your mouth or otherwise you will be taken on supprise and led out by the Klan and learnt to stretch hemp. Beware. Beware. Beware. Beware.

(Signed)

        "PHILLIP ISENBAUM,
                "*Grand Cyclops.*
        "JOHN BANKSTOWN.
        "ESAU DAVES.
        "MARCUS THOMAS.
        "BLOODY BONES.

"You know who. And all others of the Klan."

WARNING SENT BY THE KLAN

From Ku Klux Report, Alabama Testimony.

INDEX

P.

Q.

R.